The Cosmic Da

Reflections & Connections of Unified Spiritual Reality

By
Annakel Michelle

Dedication

To the seekers of truth, across all paths.

To those who find meaning in the spaces between beliefs, and to everyone who has supported me on this journey.

May this book serve as a bridge to understanding and unity.

Acknowledgements

I am deeply grateful to those who have supported me throughout the journey of writing this book.

Firstly, I want to thank Ashley M., whose guidance and wisdom have been invaluable. Your encouragement and insightful feedback have profoundly shaped this work.

A special thanks to my chosen family for their unwavering support, patience, and understanding. Your belief in me has been a constant source of strength.

Lastly, my heartfelt gratitude to all the readers and seekers of truth who inspire me to continue exploring and sharing these insights.

Thank you all for being part of this journey.

The Cosmic Dance: Divine Parallels
© 2024 by Annakel McGlinchey

All rights reserved. No part of this publication may be reproduced, distributed, or transmitted in any form or by any means, including photocopying, recording, or other electronic or mechanical methods, without the prior written permission of the publisher, except in the case of brief quotations embodied in critical reviews and certain other noncommercial uses permitted by copyright law.

ISBN: 979-8-3304-2304-0
Published by IngramSpark

Printed in United States Of America

This is a work of nonfiction. Any references to real events, places, or people are intended solely for educational purposes and are the intellectual property of the respective creators.

First Edition: September 2024

Table of Contents

Introduction 10

- The Connectedness of All Beliefs
- Engaging with Universal Truths
- Philosophical Ideas and Metaphors

Chapter 1: The Quest for Meaning 13

    Section 1.1: The Human Need for Understanding
    Section 1.2: The Role of Consciousness
    Section 1.3: Eastern and Western Approaches

Chapter 2: The Web of Beliefs 34

    Section 2.1: Myths and Narratives
    Section 2.2: Religious Doctrine and Universal Truth
    Section 2.3: Metaphor as a Bridge

Chapter 3: Metaphor and Meaning 69

    Section 3.1: The Language of Metaphor
    Section 3.2: God as a Metaphor
    Section 3.3: The Role of Symbols in Spiritual Practices

Chapter 4: From Skeptic to Seeker 96

    Section 4.1: The Journey of Doubt
    Section 4.2: Personal Transformation Through Inquiry
    Section 4.3: The Search for Universal Truth

Chapter 5: A Unified Vision of Truth 122

    Section 5.1: The One and the Many
    Section 5.2: The Role of Unity in Religion
    Section 5.3: Love as a Universal Principle

Chapter 6: The Universal Language of Spirituality 143

    Section 6.1: Spiritual Practices Across Cultures
    Section 6.2: The Sacred and the Secular
    Section 6.3: The Role of Rituals in Uniting Us

Chapter 7: Bridging the Divide 166

    Section 7.1: Overcoming Religious Conflict
    Section 7.2: Finding Common Ground
    Section 7.3: Toward a Global Ethic

Chapter 8: The Spiritual Insight of Oneness 187

Section 8.1: Mysticism and the Experience of Unity
Section 8.2: The Self and the Whole
Section 8.3: Science Meets Mysticism

Chapter 9: Living a Connected Life 207

Section 9.1: Spirituality in Everyday Life
Section 9.2: Ethical Living and the Global Community
Section 9.3: Service as Spiritual Practice

Chapter 10: Conclusion – The Infinite Journey 226

Section 10.1: Spiritual Growth as a Lifelong Path
Section 10.2: Embracing the Unknown
Section 10.3: Unity Through Diversity

Glossary 243

Bibliography/References 249

Preface

In a world rich with diverse spiritual traditions and philosophies, there remains a significant gap in how we understand and connect these different perspectives. This book was born from my observation of this gap and my desire to address it. It is my hope to offer readers a deeper understanding of spirituality and the profound ways in which we are all interconnected, despite our differing beliefs.

The goal of this work is simple yet profound: to reveal how, at the core of our varied spiritual practices and religious doctrines, there is a shared essence. By exploring the commonalities that thread through our distinct belief systems, I aim to illuminate the universal truths that unite us. Regardless of our individual paths, we are all, in essence, searching for the same fundamental truths and connections.

This book is intended for those who possess an open mind and a willingness to explore the intricate tapestry of the universe's spiritual dimensions. Whether you are curious about the broader aspects of spirituality or seeking to understand how various religions intertwine, you will find insights here that resonate with the shared human quest for meaning.

The perspective I offer is one that has seldom been articulated—an exploration of spiritual interconnectedness that seeks to bridge divides rather than accentuate them. It is an endeavor to bring forth a narrative that many have not yet fully considered, shedding light on aspects of spirituality that remain underexplored in contemporary discourse.

I am profoundly grateful to Ashley M., whose guidance and philosophical insights have been instrumental throughout my journey. Her encouragement and the depth of her own understanding have inspired me to grasp these complex concepts and integrate them into this work, even at a relatively young age.

Thank you for joining me on this exploration. May the insights within these pages foster a deeper connection to the spiritual fabric that binds us all.

Introduction

In the vast and intricate tapestry of human experience, one enduring thread consistently binds us all: the search for meaning. Across the sprawling landscapes of cultures, religions, and philosophies, there is a profound convergence in our quest for understanding. While the surface may appear diverse and fragmented, beneath it lies a remarkable unity that becomes evident when we look beyond the apparent differences.

This book embarks on an exploration of a concept that has often been overlooked or misunderstood: the deep interconnectedness of all beliefs and philosophies. At their core, every spiritual tradition, religious doctrine, and philosophical system reveals a fundamental similarity. We are all part of a grand, universal source—a collective consciousness that encompasses every deity, every human being, every thought, and every idea. This source is not confined to any singular entity but rather constitutes a vast and inclusive presence that permeates every facet of existence.

As we journey through these pages, we will unravel some of the greatest philosophical ideas and spiritual insights from a diverse array of traditions. From the contemplative practices of Eastern philosophies to the profound teachings of Western religions, from ancient wisdom to contemporary thought, our exploration will uncover the common threads that weave through our collective understanding. This book is designed to present a cohesive vision that harmonizes diverse perspectives into a unified narrative, illuminating the ways in which interconnectedness defines our shared experience. Imagine a world where every belief is not seen as an isolated viewpoint but as a reflection of a greater truth that unites us all. In this vision, the distinctions that often seem to divide us become mere surface details, while the deeper connections that bind us come into clearer focus. By embracing this perspective, we can transcend the limitations of our individual differences and foster a greater sense of empathy, unity, and mutual respect. Throughout history, great philosophers and spiritual leaders have grappled with the nature of existence and the quest for truth. This book draws upon their wisdom, integrating their insights into a comprehensive understanding of the interconnectedness of all things. We will delve into how ancient texts and modern philosophies converge on similar truths, revealing a universal thread that ties together the myriad ways in which humans seek to understand the world and their place in it.

This work is not merely an intellectual exercise; it is a heartfelt invitation to perceive the world—and ourselves—in a new and profound light. It represents an endeavor to bridge gaps, reconcile differences, and celebrate the shared essence of our spiritual and philosophical pursuits. By acknowledging and embracing the interconnectedness that defines our existence, we can cultivate a deeper appreciation for the universal source that we all share.

As you turn the pages of this book, I invite you to embark on this journey of discovery with an open mind and an open heart. May the insights you encounter inspire you to recognize the profound connections that unite us all and to embrace the universal source that binds us together.

Thank you for joining me on this exploration. Together, let us delve into the richness of our collective wisdom and uncover the unity that lies beneath the surface of our diverse beliefs and experiences.

Chapter 1: The Quest for Meaning

Section 1.1: The Human Need for Understanding

The Innate Human Drive to Seek Meaning

The quest for meaning is not merely a philosophical pursuit but a deeply embedded human trait that spans across cultures, epochs, and disciplines. Our ancestors, long before the advent of formal religion or written language, looked up at the stars, pondered the movement of the sun, and asked fundamental questions about their place in the cosmos. These early stirrings of wonder and curiosity are foundational to what it means to be human.

Aristotle and the Desire to Know

As we have already touched upon, Aristotle asserted that humans are driven by an innate desire to know. This is more than a simple curiosity; it's a profound, existential need to understand the world, our purpose, and the forces that shape our lives. This desire, Aristotle suggested, leads us to explore the causes of things, both tangible and abstract. This pursuit of knowledge is, for Aristotle, the ultimate good — one that leads to a more virtuous, contemplative life.

But Aristotle was not alone in recognizing this drive. Across the world, in different philosophical traditions, this same idea appears. In Confucianism, for example, the search for knowledge and understanding is tied to ethical conduct and social harmony. The idea is that by understanding the principles that govern the universe—whether through metaphysical inquiry, scientific exploration, or personal reflection—humans can better align their lives with these principles and live in accordance with the 'Tao' or 'way of life.'

Early Religious Responses to the Human Condition

Before formal systems of philosophy emerged, early humans sought answers to life's most profound questions through religion and mythology. At its core, religion arose as a way to understand and explain the forces beyond our control. In the absence of scientific knowledge, the world was full of mystery, danger, and uncertainty. Early humans faced natural disasters, sickness, death, and the challenges of survival without the ability to fully understand why these things happened. In their search for answers, they turned to spiritual explanations.

Across early civilizations, creation myths offered answers to the big questions: Where did we come from? Why are we here? What is the meaning of life? From the Babylonian Enuma Elish, which describes the gods shaping the earth from the chaos of primordial waters, to the ancient Egyptian creation stories where gods like Atum and Ptah gave birth to the universe, humans have always created narratives to explain existence.

Religion served another important function in answering the human need for understanding: it provided a moral and ethical framework for living. Many of the early religious systems offered not just explanations for the world's origins but also guidance on how to live a good and meaningful life. Zoroastrianism, one of the oldest monotheistic religions, introduced concepts of good and evil, emphasizing the importance of moral choice in determining one's fate in the afterlife.

Even today, religious stories and teachings continue to offer solace and a sense of purpose for millions of people worldwide. They provide answers to questions about suffering, morality, and mortality—questions that science and logic alone may never fully resolve.

The Role of Mythology: A Universal Storytelling Tool

Mythology can be seen as an early attempt to grapple with the complexities of human existence, often serving as a precursor to philosophy and religion. From the stories of Homer and the Greek myths, which sought to explain natural phenomena and human behavior through the lives of gods and heroes, to the Norse myths that conceptualized the cosmic struggle between order and chaos, myths reflect humanity's universal drive to understand.

One of the most enduring myths is that of Prometheus, who defied the gods by bringing fire to humanity, an act that symbolizes the pursuit of knowledge and enlightenment. For this transgression, Prometheus was condemned to eternal punishment, reflecting the tension between human curiosity and the dangers that come with it. This myth illustrates the paradox of knowledge: while it empowers us, it also brings unforeseen consequences, such as suffering or existential angst.

Mythologies serve another essential role: they provide moral and ethical instruction. Joseph Campbell, a scholar of comparative mythology, famously referred to myths as "the masks of God," suggesting that these stories are metaphors for the deeper truths about the universe and our place in it. Myths, then, are not merely tales of gods and heroes but reflections of our inner psychological and spiritual struggles. They offer guidance, helping us navigate life's challenges and find meaning in our experiences.

Philosophy: The Rational Response to Human Wonder

If mythology and religion answered the need for meaning through storytelling and faith, philosophy represents the rational counterpart. In the Axial Age—roughly between 800 BCE and 200 BCE—a remarkable shift occurred across multiple civilizations. This period saw the rise of great philosophical and religious traditions that continue to shape human thought today: Confucianism and Taoism in China, Buddhism and Hinduism in India, and the emergence of Greek philosophy in the West.

Philosophers like Socrates, Plato, and Aristotle in ancient Greece began to question the traditional myths and religious narratives that had dominated their cultures. Instead of relying on divine explanations, they sought to understand the world through reason and observation.

Socrates, for instance, questioned everything, famously claiming, "I know that I know nothing." This Socratic humility—that human knowledge is inherently limited—would become a cornerstone of Western philosophy.

Plato, in contrast to his teacher Socrates, developed a more structured metaphysical view of the world. In his famous allegory of the cave, Plato argued that humans are often trapped in ignorance, mistaking shadows on the wall for reality. Only through philosophical inquiry can we ascend from the cave and grasp the true nature of reality—the world of eternal forms. For Plato, the ultimate goal of philosophy was to understand the Form of the Good, the source of all meaning and value.

In India, philosophers and sages were grappling with similar questions. The Upanishads, ancient Indian texts, delved into the nature of reality and the self. They posed the idea that at the core of every being lies the Atman, or the individual soul, which is identical to Brahman, the universal soul. This notion of unity between the individual and the cosmos resonates with the idea of interconnectedness that many spiritual traditions share.

Science and the Evolution of Knowledge

As human civilization progressed, science emerged as another tool for understanding the universe. From the early astronomers of Mesopotamia and Egypt, who charted the movements of the stars, to the ancient Greek natural philosophers like Thales and Democritus, science has always been an attempt to explain the natural world through observation and experimentation.

The Scientific Revolution of the 16th and 17th centuries marked a watershed moment in this pursuit. Thinkers like Galileo, Kepler, and Newton challenged the old religious and philosophical dogmas, proposing that the universe operates according to natural laws that can be discovered through empirical inquiry. Newton's laws of motion and universal gravitation not only explained the movement of the planets but also offered a new way of thinking about the universe as a predictable, orderly system.

Yet, even as science provided answers to questions about the physical world, it also raised new questions about the nature of reality itself. The discoveries of Einstein and quantum physics in the 20th century shattered the Newtonian worldview. Suddenly, reality seemed far stranger than anyone had imagined. Quantum mechanics suggested that particles could exist in multiple states at once, and relativity revealed that space and time are interconnected and relative to the observer. These discoveries challenged our understanding of reality and raised philosophical questions about the limits of human knowledge.

As physicist Niels Bohr once remarked, "Anyone who is not shocked by quantum theory has not understood it." In many ways, the mysteries revealed by modern science echo the ancient philosophical questions about the nature of existence and the limits of human understanding.

Psychological Perspectives: The Search for Meaning and Identity

The search for meaning is not only an intellectual or spiritual pursuit but also a psychological necessity. Carl Jung, a Swiss psychiatrist and psychoanalyst, emphasized the importance of myth, religion, and symbolism in the development of the self. According to Jung, humans have a deep psychological need for meaning, which is expressed through archetypes—universal symbols that appear in dreams, myths, and religious traditions. These archetypes help individuals navigate their inner worlds and find meaning in their experiences.

Jung's concept of the collective unconscious—a shared reservoir of human experience and knowledge—suggests that the quest for meaning is not only an individual journey but also a collective one. Across cultures, people are drawn to the same symbols, stories, and ideas, all of which point to a deeper, shared reality.

Viktor Frankl, a Holocaust survivor and psychiatrist, also explored the psychological dimension of meaning in his book Man's Search for Meaning. Frankl argued that the primary drive in human life is not pleasure (as Freud suggested) but meaning. Even in the most horrific circumstances, such as his experience in Nazi concentration camps, Frankl found that those who could find meaning in their suffering were more likely to survive. For Frankl, meaning is not something we passively discover but something we actively create through our choices and actions.

In these many expressions of the human search for meaning—whether through religion, mythology, philosophy, science, or psychology—the same fundamental questions emerge: What is the nature of reality? What is our place in the universe? What does it mean to live a good life? These questions have haunted humanity for millennia and continue to drive us forward in our quest for understanding. The answers may never be fully known, but the journey itself—the search for truth, purpose, and meaning—is what defines us as human beings.

Section 1.2 The Role of Consciousness

Descartes and the Birth of Modern Consciousness

René Descartes' famous assertion, "Cogito, ergo sum"—translated as "I think, therefore I am"—marks a pivotal moment in Western philosophy. This deceptively simple statement anchors modern thought by centering self-awareness as the foundation of all certainty. Descartes' reasoning is straightforward but revolutionary: even if all external reality could be doubted, the fact that he could doubt, question, or think about his existence meant that there was something undeniable—the existence of the thinking self. The act of thinking, in all its forms—doubting, questioning, imagining, believing—demonstrates the undeniable truth of one's own existence.

Descartes' insight launched a new way of understanding human consciousness and its relationship to knowledge. Before him, much of medieval philosophy was grounded in theological or external authority, often relying on religious texts or external observation to define reality. Descartes turned inward, emphasizing the importance of the subjective self in constructing knowledge. His focus on consciousness, and the idea that our inner awareness of thought is the most certain reality, set the stage for the development of rationalism. From this point, philosophy began to consider not only the external world but also the internal world of the mind as equally, if not more, significant in the quest for knowledge and meaning.

The implications of Descartes' declaration have rippled through centuries of philosophical discourse, influencing how we view the mind, the self, and the search for truth. Descartes proposed that self-awareness is the very essence of our being and that from this conscious experience, we can begin to investigate and understand the nature of reality.

Consciousness: The Mirror of Reality

Consciousness, the inner life of thought and awareness, serves as a mirror that reflects our experiences, enabling us to interpret and make sense of the world around us. Without it, we would be no more than biological automatons, reacting to stimuli without reflection, insight, or intention. It is consciousness that allows us to ask questions about the universe, to wonder about our place in it, and to search for meaning.

The concept of consciousness has fascinated philosophers for centuries, not just because of its existence, but because of the mystery surrounding it. How do we experience the world? Why are we able to reflect on our thoughts and emotions, while other creatures seem only to react? Consciousness is a distinctly human trait, enabling us to transcend basic survival instincts and ask deeper, more profound questions about existence. This ability to be aware of oneself and the world forms the basis of all philosophy and religious thought.

Through consciousness, humans can ask fundamental questions about existence that go beyond survival: What is reality? What is the meaning of life? What is the nature of truth? These questions would not be possible without the inner life that consciousness provides. It allows us to look at ourselves, not as isolated entities, but as beings in relation to others, the world, and the cosmos itself.

Descartes' idea of consciousness as the seat of certainty still influences modern thought, though with a more nuanced understanding of how consciousness works. Instead of seeing consciousness merely as a solitary experience of self-awareness, modern thought explores how our consciousness is shaped by our interactions with the world, other people, and our broader cultural and environmental context. While Descartes saw consciousness as primarily a solitary process, today we understand it as a dynamic interplay between self and world.

Eastern Philosophies: Consciousness as Unity

While Western philosophy, particularly in the wake of Descartes, often emphasizes the role of individual consciousness in the search for meaning, Eastern philosophies offer a different perspective—one that sees consciousness not as an individual experience but as a universal one. The difference in approach to consciousness between Eastern and Western traditions reveals rich, complementary ways of understanding our relationship to reality.

In Advaita Vedanta, an important school of Hindu philosophy, consciousness is viewed as universal. It posits that the individual self (Atman) is not separate from the ultimate reality of the universe (Brahman), but rather a manifestation of it. This teaching asserts that the perception of separation between individual consciousness and the cosmos is an illusion (maya). The goal of spiritual practice is to realize the unity of the individual soul with the greater cosmic consciousness—a realization known as Moksha or liberation.

Similarly, in Buddhism, consciousness plays a central role in the quest for enlightenment, but rather than emphasizing self-awareness in a personal, individualistic sense, Buddhism focuses on transcending the ego. The Buddhist path encourages practitioners to see through the illusion of the self and recognize that all things are interconnected. In the state of Nirvana, the mind is liberated from the cycle of craving and suffering, revealing the truth of unity with all existence. Consciousness, from this perspective, is a means to perceive the impermanent and interconnected nature of reality, rather than as a separate, enduring self.

These Eastern traditions offer a vision of consciousness that contrasts with the Western focus on individualism and personal identity. They suggest that consciousness is not something that belongs to "me" alone, but rather is a part of the greater whole. From this view, the ultimate goal is not to strengthen or glorify personal consciousness but to dissolve the illusion of separateness and realize the unity of all things.

Consciousness and the Scientific Perspective

In the modern scientific world, consciousness remains one of the greatest mysteries. While neuroscience has made enormous strides in understanding how the brain works—mapping the neural correlates of consciousness, identifying the regions of the brain responsible for self-awareness and sensory experience—the essential nature of consciousness remains elusive. The central question that continues to puzzle scientists is: How does subjective experience arise from the physical brain?

This is the so-called "hard problem of consciousness," as coined by philosopher David Chalmers. While scientists can explain how certain brain processes correspond to certain states of consciousness—like how electrical activity in the brain results in visual experiences or how neurons fire when we recall a memory—they have not yet been able to explain why or how these processes create subjective experience. Why does the arrangement of atoms and molecules in the brain give rise to awareness? This gap between the physical brain and the lived experience of consciousness is one of the great unsolved puzzles of our time.

Some philosophers and scientists argue that consciousness might be an irreducible aspect of the universe, much like space, time, and matter. This viewpoint, called panpsychism, suggests that consciousness might be a fundamental feature of reality, present in all things to varying degrees, rather than an emergent property that only arises in highly complex systems like the human brain.

Quantum mechanics, with its strange and counterintuitive discoveries, has also contributed to debates about consciousness. The famous "double-slit experiment" in quantum physics, for example, shows that the mere act of observation can change the behavior of particles. Some interpretations suggest that consciousness itself may play a role in shaping reality, leading to the idea that the mind and the physical world may be more intertwined than we previously thought. Though this idea remains speculative, it opens the door to new ways of thinking about the relationship between consciousness and the nature of the universe.

Philosophical Debates: Consciousness and Free Will

Consciousness is also at the heart of debates about free will, personal responsibility, and ethics. Friedrich Nietzsche, for instance, challenged the traditional views of consciousness and free will by suggesting that human beings are driven by unconscious forces—instincts, desires, and a will to power—that lie beyond rational thought. Nietzsche's philosophy emphasized that much of what we think of as "conscious" decisions is actually shaped by deeper, hidden motivations that we may not be aware of. This raises questions about the degree to which humans are truly in control of their actions.

In contrast, Jean-Paul Sartre, one of the leading existentialists, placed consciousness and free will at the very center of his philosophy. Sartre famously argued that human beings are radically free, and that consciousness is what allows us to transcend external circumstances and define our own existence. According to Sartre, we are not born with a predetermined essence; rather, we create ourselves through our choices and actions. However, this freedom also comes with the weight of responsibility—because we are free, we must take full responsibility for our lives and the meaning we create.

Sartre's philosophy of existentialism highlights the role of consciousness in making choices and constructing meaning. It is through our awareness of our freedom that we realize the need to create meaning in a world that does not offer any inherent answers. This freedom, while liberating, can also be overwhelming—what Sartre called the "anguish" of existence. Consciousness, therefore, is not only the source of freedom but also the source of our existential dilemmas.

Consciousness as the Key to the Future of Humanity

As we move into an age defined by rapid technological advancements, the question of consciousness becomes more pressing than ever. Fields such as artificial intelligence and neuroscience are beginning to challenge our traditional notions of what it means to be conscious and what it means to be human. If machines can develop a form of self-awareness, what would that mean for our understanding of the mind? If we could upload consciousness into a digital form, would that still be "us"?

The future of consciousness studies will likely redefine what it means to be human and challenge us to rethink the boundaries of identity, free will, and meaning. Consciousness is at the heart of these existential questions, and the answers we discover—or fail to discover—will shape the future of philosophy, science, and humanity.

In summary, consciousness is the foundation of all human experience, the mirror through which we perceive and understand reality. Whether viewed through the lens of Western philosophy's focus on individual thought, Eastern spirituality's recognition of unity, or modern science's quest to understand the brain, consciousness remains the ultimate mystery and the key to unlocking the deepest questions of existence. It is through consciousness that we find the pathway to meaning, freedom, and connection with the universe.

Section 1.3: Eastern and Western Approaches

Interconnectedness vs. Individualism: Two Paths to Meaning

Human beings across cultures have sought answers to fundamental questions about life, existence, and meaning. However, the frameworks through which these questions are approached can vary widely depending on cultural, religious, and philosophical traditions. Two dominant schools of thought—Eastern and Western philosophy—offer contrasting yet complementary perspectives on the nature of self, reality, and the pursuit of meaning.

The Eastern approach, embodied in traditions such as Buddhism, Hinduism, and Taoism, emphasizes interconnectedness and the dissolution of the ego in order to achieve unity with the greater whole. In contrast,

Western philosophy, particularly through schools like existentialism and stoicism, tends to emphasize individualism, personal responsibility, and the development of the self. These two philosophical currents offer unique pathways toward finding truth, fulfillment, and peace, but they approach the role of the self in profoundly different ways.

Eastern Philosophy: Interconnectedness and the Dissolution of the Self

One of the most central themes in Eastern philosophy is the notion of interconnectedness. In traditions like Buddhism, Hinduism, and Taoism, the boundaries between the individual and the cosmos are seen as illusions, and the pursuit of wisdom often involves realizing this essential unity.

Buddhism: The Interconnectedness of All Beings

In Buddhism, the concept of dependent origination (also known as pratītyasamutpāda) teaches that all things arise in dependence upon other things. Nothing exists independently or in isolation; instead, everything is interdependent. This concept applies not only to physical phenomena but also to the human experience of suffering, desire, and identity. According to the Buddha, suffering arises from our attachment to the self, our belief that we are independent and separate entities. Enlightenment, or Nirvana, is attained when one realizes the impermanence and interconnectedness of all things, thereby transcending the illusion of the self and the cycles of craving and suffering.

In this framework, personal fulfillment comes not from asserting one's individuality or ego, but from letting go of it. The path to meaning in Buddhism lies in understanding that the self is an illusion created by attachment and desire. By releasing the ego and embracing the interconnectedness of all things, one can attain peace, wisdom, and a deeper connection with the universe.

Buddhist teachings on interdependence extend not only to the spiritual realm but also to ethical behavior. The recognition that all beings are interconnected leads to compassion for others, as one sees their suffering as intimately tied to one's own. This compassionate outlook encourages mindfulness, ethical behavior, and the pursuit of spiritual growth, not just for the individual but for the benefit of all beings.

Hinduism: Unity with Brahman

Hinduism, another major Eastern tradition, similarly teaches that the self (Atman) is not truly separate from the universe but is, in fact, a manifestation of the ultimate reality, Brahman. Brahman is the eternal, unchanging source of all that exists, and the realization of one's unity with Brahman is considered the highest spiritual goal in Hinduism.

In Hindu philosophy, the perception of individuality and separateness is considered part of the maya, or illusion, that veils the true nature of reality. Liberation, known as Moksha, is achieved when an individual realizes that their true self, the Atman, is identical to Brahman. This realization brings about freedom from the cycle of samsara—the endless cycle of birth, death, and rebirth—and the suffering that accompanies it.

In this context, the search for meaning is not an outward quest but an inward journey. The individual's task is to dissolve the false sense of separateness, to see through the veil of maya, and to reconnect with the ultimate, universal consciousness. The notion of interconnectedness in Hinduism is profound, linking not only all living beings but also the divine, the natural world, and the cosmos.

Taoism: Flowing with the Tao

Taoism, an ancient Chinese philosophy, also emphasizes the interconnectedness of all things through the concept of the Tao. The Tao, often translated as "the Way," is the underlying principle of the universe. It is the source and force that flows through all life and connects everything. Taoism teaches that individuals should strive to live in harmony with the Tao by embracing the natural flow of life and relinquishing their efforts to control or dominate their environment.

In Taoist thought, the self is not viewed as an isolated individual but as part of the greater whole. Taoism encourages the practice of wu wei, or "non-action," which means aligning oneself with the natural currents of life and responding to situations in a way that is effortless and spontaneous, rather than forced or contrived. The idea is that, by flowing with the Tao, one can find peace and meaning in a world that is inherently dynamic and ever-changing.

In contrast to Western notions of individualism and self-determination, Taoism teaches that the self is a part of the larger cosmic process. By surrendering control and recognizing the interdependence of all things, individuals can achieve harmony, both within themselves and with the world around them.

Western Philosophy: Individualism and the Power of the Self

While Eastern philosophies tend to focus on dissolving the ego and recognizing interconnectedness, Western philosophies often emphasize the importance of the individual and the development of personal responsibility. This focus on individualism is evident in schools of thought such as existentialism and stoicism, both of which place the individual at the center of the search for meaning and truth.

Existentialism: Radical Freedom and Responsibility

Existentialism, a 20th-century Western philosophical movement, focuses heavily on the individual's subjective experience and the quest for personal meaning. For existentialists like Jean-Paul Sartre, Simone de Beauvoir, and Friedrich Nietzsche, the world has no inherent meaning or purpose; instead, meaning is something that must be created by the individual through their choices and actions.

Sartre famously declared, "Existence precedes essence," meaning that human beings are not born with a preordained purpose or nature. Rather, we exist first, and it is through our conscious choices that we define who we are. This emphasis on individual freedom places great responsibility on the self, as Sartre asserts that humans are "condemned to be free." With this radical freedom comes the burden of shaping one's own life without relying on external authorities, whether religious, social, or philosophical.

In existentialism, the search for meaning is an inherently personal endeavor. There is no universal truth or connection waiting to be discovered; instead, each person must face the absurdity of existence and craft meaning from within. This focus on individualism stands in stark contrast to the Eastern emphasis on interconnectedness, as existentialists reject the idea that there is an underlying unity to all things. Instead, they argue that humans must create meaning in a world that is indifferent or even hostile to their desires.

While this can seem isolating, existentialists also argue that it is empowering. The ability to define one's own existence, free from the constraints of external forces, allows individuals to achieve true authenticity. Nietzsche, for example, called for the emergence of the Übermensch (Overman or Superman), an individual who creates their own values and lives life on their own terms, free from the moral constraints of society or religion.

Stoicism: Mastery of the Self

Where existentialism emphasizes freedom and personal choice, Stoicism—a much older Western tradition, originating in ancient Greece—focuses on the cultivation of self-control and resilience in the face of external circumstances. Founded by Zeno of Citium and later developed by philosophers such as Epictetus, Seneca, and Marcus Aurelius, Stoicism teaches that the key to a meaningful life is mastering one's emotions and desires.

Stoicism holds that while we cannot control the external world or the events that happen to us, we can control our responses to them. The Stoics encourage individuals to cultivate virtue (especially wisdom, courage, justice, and temperance) as the highest good and to accept the natural order of the universe. In this way, Stoicism teaches individuals to find peace and contentment not by changing the world but by changing themselves.

The Stoic philosophy of amor fati, or "love of fate," encourages individuals to embrace everything that happens in life, even hardship and suffering, as necessary parts of existence. By accepting what cannot be changed and focusing on what is within one's control, the Stoic finds meaning and tranquility even in adversity.

While Stoicism emphasizes self-mastery and individual virtue, it does not deny the interconnectedness of all things. The Stoics believed in a cosmopolitan worldview, which held that all humans are part of a single community bound by shared reason and natural law. In this way, Stoicism blends individual responsibility with a broader recognition of the interdependence of all people.

Synthesis: Two Paths, One Goal

Despite the differences between Eastern and Western approaches, both ultimately seek to answer the same fundamental questions about the nature of existence, the self, and the meaning of life. Eastern philosophy tends to view meaning as something that comes from recognizing our interconnectedness with the universe and dissolving the illusion of the self, while Western philosophy often views meaning as something that the individual must create through personal freedom, responsibility, and self-mastery.

However, these approaches are not necessarily contradictory. They can be seen as complementary pathways to truth and fulfillment.

Chapter 2: The Web of Beliefs

Section 2.1: Shared Stories and Narratives

Introduction: The Power of Stories

Since the dawn of humanity, shared stories and narratives have been fundamental tools for understanding the world, conveying cultural values, and shaping belief systems. Passed down through generations, these stories serve as vessels for collective wisdom, moral lessons, and explanations of natural phenomena. They provide frameworks for societies to interpret their experiences and define their place in the cosmos.

These narratives are more than mere tales; they are symbolic expressions that delve into the fundamental aspects of human existence—life and death, good and evil, the nature of the soul, and the mysteries of the universe. Through shared stories, ancient peoples articulated their understanding of reality, codified their values, and connected with the divine. Their true power lies in the underlying truths they reveal about the human condition.

This section explores how shared stories and religious narratives shape belief systems by examining the ideas of Joseph Campbell and Carl Jung. Their work reveals that despite cultural differences, there are universal patterns and archetypes in these stories that reflect shared human experiences and truths.

Joseph Campbell and the Hero's Journey

The Monomyth: A Universal Pattern

Joseph Campbell, an American mythologist, writer, and lecturer, profoundly impacted the understanding of stories through his concept of the "monomyth," or the "hero's journey." In his seminal work, *The Hero with a Thousand Faces*, Campbell argues that many of the world's narratives share a fundamental structure. This universal pattern transcends cultural and historical boundaries, suggesting a shared human experience encoded in our stories.

The hero's journey typically involves several key stages:

1. **The Call to Adventure**: The hero begins in the ordinary world but receives a call to enter an unknown realm filled with challenges.
2. **The Threshold**: The hero crosses into the new world, often encountering a mentor or guide.
3. **Trials and Challenges**: The hero faces a series of tests, allies, and enemies that prepare them for the ultimate ordeal.
4. **The Abyss or Revelation**: The hero confronts their greatest fear or enemy, leading to a transformative experience.
5. **The Return**: The hero returns to the ordinary world with new wisdom or power that benefits their community.

Campbell's monomyth illustrates that despite the diversity of stories across cultures, there is a common narrative thread that reflects the psychological and spiritual development of individuals. The hero's journey serves as a metaphor for personal growth, transformation, and the quest for self-actualization.

Stories as Mirrors of the Human Psyche

Campbell believed that shared stories are symbolic expressions of the inner workings of the human mind. They externalize our internal struggles, desires, and fears, allowing us to confront and understand them. The hero's journey represents the universal process of individuation—the journey toward becoming a whole, integrated person.

For example, in Greek narratives, the story of Theseus and the Minotaur symbolizes the confrontation with one's inner demons. Theseus enters the labyrinth (the subconscious mind) to slay the Minotaur (his fears and primal instincts). Upon success, he emerges transformed, embodying courage and wisdom.

In Star Wars, a modern narrative heavily influenced by Campbell's work, Luke Skywalker's journey mirrors the hero's journey template. Luke receives the call to adventure, faces trials, confronts his inner darkness and external enemies, and returns empowered to aid his community.

By identifying these patterns, Campbell demonstrated that shared stories are not just cultural artifacts but expressions of universal human experiences and psychological truths.

Carl Jung and Archetypes

The Collective Unconscious

Swiss psychiatrist Carl Gustav Jung introduced the concept of the collective unconscious, a part of the unconscious mind containing memories and behavioral patterns inherited from past generations. According to Jung, the collective unconscious is universal and shared by all humans, comprising innate predispositions known as archetypes.

Archetypes are primordial images and symbols that recur across cultures and time periods. They manifest in dreams, stories, art, and religious narratives, representing fundamental human motifs such as the hero, the mother, the trickster, and the shadow.

Archetypes in Shared Stories and Narratives

Jung identified several key archetypes commonly found in shared stories:

1. **The Hero**: Symbolizes the ego and the quest for identity and wholeness. The hero's journey reflects the struggle to overcome obstacles and achieve personal growth.

2. **The Mentor**: Represents wisdom and guidance. Characters like Merlin in Arthurian legends or Yoda in Star Wars embody this archetype.
3. **The Shadow**: Represents the unconscious, repressed aspects of the self. Confronting the shadow is essential for personal integration.
4. **The Anima and Animus**: Represent the feminine and masculine aspects within an individual, guiding the integration of these dualities.
5. **The Self**: Symbolizes the unified unconscious and conscious mind, achieved through the process of individuation.

By recognizing these archetypes in narratives, Jung argued that these stories are expressions of universal psychological processes. They provide a means for individuals to navigate their inner worlds and achieve psychological integration.

Stories as Tools for Self-Understanding

Jung believed that engaging with shared stories and archetypal symbols facilitates personal growth. Narratives offer a framework for individuals to understand their experiences, emotions, and behaviors. They act as mirrors, reflecting internal conflicts and guiding individuals toward self-awareness.

For instance, the story of Persephone's descent into the underworld can be seen as an archetype for facing and integrating one's shadow aspects. Persephone's journey represents the necessity of confronting darkness to achieve rebirth and transformation.

Transcending Cultural Boundaries

Universal Themes in Shared Stories

Despite vast cultural differences, many narratives share common themes and motifs. This universality suggests that stories tap into fundamental aspects of the human experience. Themes such as the creation of the world, great floods, trickster figures, and journeys to the underworld appear in diverse cultures:

- **Creation Stories**: Nearly every culture has a narrative explaining the origins of the universe and humanity. These stories address existential questions about existence and purpose.

- **Flood Narratives**: Accounts of a great flood, like those in the Epic of Gilgamesh or the Biblical story of Noah's Ark, reflect themes of destruction and renewal.
- **The Trickster**: Characters like Loki in Norse legends or Anansi in African tales embody chaos and change, challenging the status quo and prompting transformation.

These recurring themes highlight shared human concerns and the collective effort to understand life's mysteries.

Stories and Moral Frameworks

Shared stories often serve as moral guides, teaching values and ethical principles. They illustrate consequences of actions, reinforce societal norms, and explore complex moral dilemmas. For example:

- **The Story of King Midas**: Teaches about greed and the unintended consequences of one's desires.
- **The Tale of the Prodigal Son**: Explores themes of forgiveness, redemption, and unconditional love.

By embedding moral lessons within engaging narratives, stories effectively transmit cultural values across generations.

The Role of Shared Stories in Shaping Belief Systems

Foundations of Religion and Spirituality

Shared stories form the backbone of many religious traditions, providing the narratives that underpin beliefs, rituals, and practices. They offer explanations for the origins of the universe, the nature of the divine, and the relationship between the sacred and humanity.

In Hinduism, the epics Mahabharata and Ramayana are rich with narratives that convey philosophical teachings and ethical guidelines. The Bhagavad Gita, part of the Mahabharata, addresses the moral struggle of duty versus personal desire.

In Native American traditions, shared stories explain natural phenomena and convey the sacredness of the land. Stories of the Great Spirit and creation narratives reinforce the interconnectedness of all life.

Cultural Identity and Cohesion

Shared stories contribute to a shared cultural identity by providing common narratives that unify a community. They reinforce social structures, traditions, and collective values. Festivals, rituals, and ceremonies often reenact significant stories, strengthening communal bonds.

For example, the Japanese story of Amaterasu, the sun goddess, is central to Shinto beliefs and the imperial lineage. Rituals and traditions stemming from this narrative reinforce national identity and cultural heritage.

Adaptation and Evolution of Stories

Shared stories are not static; they evolve over time, adapting to changing cultural contexts. Modern storytelling mediums—literature, film, and television—continue to draw on traditional themes and archetypes.

The popularity of superhero narratives in contemporary culture reflects modern reinterpretations of the hero's journey. Characters like Superman and Wonder Woman embody timeless archetypes, addressing contemporary issues while connecting to ancient patterns.

Conclusion: Shared Stories as Universal Bridges

Shared stories and narratives are powerful tools that shape belief systems by encapsulating universal truths within culturally specific contexts. The work of Joseph Campbell and Carl Jung illuminates how these narratives, through shared patterns and archetypes, transcend cultural boundaries and tap into the collective human psyche.

By studying these stories, we gain insight into the fundamental concerns and aspirations that unite humanity. They reveal that despite our diverse cultures and histories, we share common questions, fears, and hopes. Shared stories encourage us to explore our inner worlds, understand our place in the universe, and connect with others across time and space.

Engaging with these narratives enriches our understanding of ourselves and others, fostering empathy, wisdom, and a deeper appreciation for the shared human journey.

Section 2.2: Religious Doctrine and Universal Truth

Introduction: The Quest for the Divine

Throughout human history, the search for understanding the nature of the divine and our connection to it has been a central preoccupation of civilizations across the globe. Religions have emerged as systems of belief that not only provide explanations for the mysteries of existence but also offer pathways for individuals to connect with something greater than themselves. Despite the vast diversity of religious doctrines, rituals, and practices, a common thread weaves through them all: the recognition of a transcendent reality and the inherent connection between the divine and humanity.

In this section, we will explore how various religions—Christianity, Islam, Judaism, Buddhism, Hinduism, Sikhism, Taoism, and others—interpret the nature of the divine and our relationship with it. By examining these interpretations, we will uncover the universal truths that transcend specific doctrines, highlighting the shared human yearning to understand and unite with the greater whole.

Christianity: Union with God Through Love and Redemption

The Nature of the Divine

Christianity centers on the belief in one God who exists as a Trinity—Father, Son (Jesus Christ), and Holy Spirit. This doctrine emphasizes a God who is both transcendent and immanent:

- Transcendent: God is above and beyond the physical universe, infinite and eternal.
- Immanent: God is present within creation and accessible to humanity.

God is characterized by attributes such as love, mercy, justice, and omnipotence. The divine is not an abstract force but a personal being who desires a relationship with humanity.

Human Connection to the Divine

Christian doctrine teaches that humans are created in the image of God (*Imago Dei*), which signifies a special relationship between the divine and humanity. This concept implies that humans possess inherent dignity, moral capacity, and the ability to engage in a personal relationship with God.

Original Sin and Redemption:

- Original Sin: Humanity's fall from grace due to disobedience (the story of Adam and Eve) introduced sin into the world, creating a separation between humans and God.
- Redemption Through Jesus Christ: Christians believe that Jesus, the Son of God, became incarnate to reconcile humanity with God. Through his life, death, and resurrection, he provides a path for salvation.

Union with God

The ultimate goal in Christianity is to achieve union with God, which is facilitated through:

- Faith: Belief in God and acceptance of Jesus as Savior.
- Grace: The unmerited favor of God that enables humans to overcome sin.

- Love: The greatest commandment is to love God and love one's neighbor.

This union is both a present reality and a future hope, culminating in eternal life with God.

Islam: Submission to the Will of Allah

The Nature of the Divine

In Islam, God (Allah) is strictly monotheistic:

- Tawhid: The oneness and uniqueness of Allah.
- Attributes of Allah: Compassionate, merciful, just, omnipotent, and omniscient.

Allah is transcendent yet intimately involved in the affairs of the universe.

Human Connection to the Divine

Humans are considered the vicegerents (khalifah) of Allah on earth, entrusted with the responsibility to care for creation.

Submission and Obedience:

- Islam means "submission" or "surrender" to the will of Allah.
- The purpose of life is to worship Allah and follow His guidance as revealed in the Qur'an and exemplified by the Prophet Muhammad.

The Path to Unity with Allah

Union with the divine is achieved through:

- Five Pillars of Islam: Declaration of faith, prayer, almsgiving, fasting, and pilgrimage.
- Living Righteously: Following Sharia (Islamic law) and practicing virtues like honesty, compassion, and justice.
- Remembrance of Allah (Dhikr): Constant mindfulness of God in daily life.

The concept of Taqwa (God-consciousness) emphasizes an ongoing awareness of Allah's presence, guiding ethical conduct and spiritual growth.

Judaism: Covenant and Holiness

The Nature of the Divine

Judaism is based on the belief in one, indivisible God who is the creator and sustainer of the universe.

- YHWH (Yahweh): The sacred name of God, often considered too holy to pronounce.
- Attributes: Just, merciful, omnipotent, and intimately involved in history.

God is both transcendent and immanent, engaging with humanity through covenants.

Human Connection to the Divine

The Covenant Relationship:

- Abrahamic Covenant: God establishes a special relationship with Abraham and his descendants.
- Sinai Covenant: God gives the Torah (law) to Moses, outlining the commandments and expectations.

Humans are called to be partners with God in the pursuit of justice and holiness.

Living in Relationship with God

Union with the divine is expressed through:

- Observance of the Torah: Adherence to commandments governing ethical behavior, rituals, and social justice.
- Prayer and Worship: Regular prayer, study of sacred texts, and participation in communal worship.
- Pursuit of Tikkun Olam: The concept of "repairing the world" emphasizes social responsibility and making the world a better place.

Judaism focuses on action and ethical living as means to connect with God and fulfill one's purpose.

Buddhism: The Path to Enlightenment and the Interconnectedness of All

The Nature of the Divine

Buddhism differs from theistic religions in that it does not center on a creator God. Instead, it focuses on understanding the nature of reality and the mind.

- Buddha Nature: The inherent potential for enlightenment present in all beings.
- Interdependent Origination: All phenomena arise in dependence upon multiple causes and conditions.

Human Connection to the Ultimate Reality

The ultimate goal is to achieve Nirvana, a state of liberation from suffering and the cycle of rebirth (Samsara).

Four Noble Truths:

1. Dukkha: The truth of suffering.
2. Samudaya: The cause of suffering is desire and attachment.
3. Nirodha: The cessation of suffering is possible.
4. Magga: The path leading to the cessation of suffering is the Eightfold Path.

The Path to Enlightenment

The Eightfold Path provides a practical guide:

1. Right Understanding
2. Right Intent
3. Right Speech
4. Right Action
5. Right Livelihood
6. Right Effort
7. Right Mindfulness
8. Right Concentration

By cultivating wisdom, ethical conduct, and mental discipline, individuals can realize the interconnectedness of all life and attain enlightenment.

Mahayana Buddhism introduces the concept of the Bodhisattva, an enlightened being who postpones Nirvana to help others achieve liberation, emphasizing compassion and interconnectedness.

Hinduism: Unity with the Ultimate Reality (Brahman)

The Nature of the Divine

Hinduism is complex, with beliefs ranging from monotheism to polytheism and pantheism.

- Brahman: The ultimate, unchanging reality, pure consciousness, and bliss.
- Atman: The individual soul or self, which is ultimately identical to Brahman.

Gods and goddesses (e.g., Brahma, Vishnu, Shiva, Durga) represent various aspects of the divine and the functions of the universe.

Human Connection to the Divine

The fundamental teaching is that the Atman (individual soul) is one with Brahman (universal soul).

Maya and Samsara:

- Maya: The illusion of separateness and the material world.
- Samsara: The cycle of birth, death, and rebirth driven by karma (actions and their consequences).

Paths to Realization (Moksha)

Liberation (Moksha) from Samsara is achieved through:

- Jnana Yoga: The path of knowledge and wisdom.
- Bhakti Yoga: The path of devotion and love towards a personal deity.
- Karma Yoga: The path of selfless action without attachment to results.
- Raja Yoga: The path of meditation and mental discipline.

These paths guide individuals toward realizing their true nature as one with Brahman, transcending the illusion of separateness.

Sikhism: Oneness of God and Equality of Humanity

The Nature of the Divine

Sikhism teaches belief in one God (Waheguru), who is:

- Nirankar: Formless.
- Akal: Eternal.
- Kartapurakh: The creator being involved in the world.

God is both transcendent and immanent, pervading all creation.

Human Connection to the Divine

Humans have the potential to merge with God through devotion and righteous living.

Key Concepts:

- Naam: The divine name; meditating on God's name is central to spiritual practice.
- Hukam: Divine will; living in harmony with God's will leads to peace.

The Path to Union with God

Union is pursued through:

- Simran: Remembrance of God through meditation and chanting.
- Seva: Selfless service to others.
- Living Virtuously: Emphasizing honesty, compassion, humility, and equality.

Sikhism rejects caste distinctions and promotes the equality of all humans, reflecting the belief in the divine spark within everyone.

Taoism (Daoism): Harmony with the Tao

The Nature of the Divine

In Taoism, the Tao (Dao) is the ultimate reality and source of all existence:

- Tao: Literally "The Way"; an ineffable, eternal principle that underlies the universe.
- Wu Wei: Action through non-action; aligning with the natural flow.

The Tao is not a personal god but an impersonal force that cannot be fully described or conceptualized.

Human Connection to the Tao

Humans are an integral part of the Tao and can achieve harmony by aligning themselves with its principles.

Key Concepts:

- Naturalness (Ziran): Embracing one's true nature and spontaneity.
- Simplicity: Reducing desires and living modestly.
- Compassion, Moderation, Humility: The three treasures guiding ethical behavior.

The Path of Harmony

Practices include:

- Meditation and Qigong: Cultivating internal energy and tranquility.
- Observation of Nature: Learning from the patterns and rhythms of the natural world.
- Balance of Yin and Yang: Recognizing the complementary forces in the universe.

By embodying these principles, individuals align with the Tao, achieving peace and fulfillment.

Common Themes Across Religions

Despite differences in doctrines and practices, several universal themes emerge:

Transcendence and Immanence

- Transcendence: Recognition of a reality beyond the physical world.
- Immanence: Belief that the divine is present within the world and accessible to humans.

The Human-Divine Connection

- Image of God (Christianity, Judaism, Islam): Humans reflect divine attributes.
- Divine Spark (Sikhism, Hinduism): The presence of the divine within each person.
- Buddha Nature (Buddhism): Inherent potential for enlightenment.

The Illusion of Separateness

- Maya (Hinduism): Illusion that hides the true unity of existence.
- Ego and Attachment (Buddhism): Sources of suffering that obscure interconnectedness.
- Sin and Separation (Christianity): Actions that create distance from God.

Paths to Union or Liberation

- Faith and Devotion: Emphasized in Christianity, Islam, Sikhism, and Bhakti Yoga (Hinduism).
- Ethical Living and Virtue: Central to all religions, guiding moral conduct.
- Meditation and Mindfulness: Practiced in Buddhism, Hinduism, Taoism, and contemplative traditions in Christianity and Islam.
- Knowledge and Wisdom: Pursued through study, reflection, and discernment.

Compassion and Service

- Love Thy Neighbor (Christianity)
- Compassion for All Beings (Buddhism)
- Seva (Sikhism)
- Charity (Islam's Zakat)
- Tikkun Olam (Judaism)

These principles emphasize caring for others as an expression of divine connection.

The Universal Truth: Part of Something Greater

At the core of these diverse religious traditions lies a profound acknowledgment that humans are part of something greater than themselves. This greater reality may be understood as:

- A Personal God: Engaging in relationships with humanity.
- An Ultimate Reality or Principle: Underlying and unifying all existence.
- A Cosmic Order: Governed by laws and interconnected forces.

Implications of This Universal Truth:

1. Interconnectedness: Recognizing that all life is interconnected fosters empathy and responsibility toward others and the environment.
2. Transcendence of the Self: Moving beyond ego-centric perspectives to embrace a broader identity.
3. Purpose and Meaning: Finding meaning in aligning one's life with higher principles or divine will.
4. Ethical Imperative: Motivated by the understanding that actions have far-reaching consequences, ethical behavior becomes a spiritual necessity.

5. Hope and Comfort: Belief in a greater reality provides solace in the face of suffering and uncertainty.

Bridging Differences Through Shared Understanding

By exploring the commonalities among religions, we can:

- Promote Interfaith Dialogue: Encouraging mutual respect and learning.
- Foster Peace and Cooperation: Recognizing shared values reduces conflict.
- Enrich Personal Spirituality: Learning from diverse traditions can deepen one's own faith or understanding.

Challenges:

- Dogmatism: Rigid adherence to doctrines can hinder appreciation of others.
- Misinterpretation: Lack of understanding can lead to prejudice or fear.

Opportunities:

- Education: Promotes awareness and dispels misconceptions.
- Shared Initiatives: Collaborative efforts on social issues reflect common ethical commitments.

Conclusion: Embracing the Greater Whole

The exploration of religious doctrines reveals that while the paths may differ, the destination is remarkably similar. Humanity's quest to understand the divine and our place in the universe leads us toward the recognition of a greater reality that encompasses us all. This universal truth invites us to transcend individual differences, embrace our shared humanity, and contribute to the flourishing of all beings.

By acknowledging that we are all part of something greater, we open ourselves to deeper connections—with the divine, with each other, and with the world. This realization can inspire us to live with greater compassion, purpose, and harmony, fulfilling the highest aspirations of our varied but fundamentally united spiritual heritage.

Section 2.3: Metaphor as a Bridge

Introduction: The Power of Metaphor in Spiritual Language

Language is a fundamental tool through which humans attempt to understand and communicate complex and abstract concepts. In the realm of spirituality and religion, language often grapples with describing the ineffable—the ultimate reality, the divine, or the transcendent. Metaphor becomes an indispensable vehicle in this endeavor, allowing us to express ideas that are beyond literal comprehension. Philosophers and theologians like Paul Tillich have argued that all religious language is inherently symbolic or metaphorical. This section explores how metaphors in spiritual texts serve as bridges, connecting diverse religious expressions to a unified, universal source, even when articulated differently.

Paul Tillich and the Symbolic Nature of Religious Language

Tillich's Theology of Symbol

Tillich's perspective suggests that:

- **All Religious Language is Symbolic**: Statements about God or the ultimate concern are not literal descriptions but symbolic expressions pointing beyond themselves.
- **Avoiding Idolatry**: Taking metaphors literally leads to idolatry—confusing the symbol with the reality it represents.
- **Universal Accessibility**: Because symbols tap into universal human experiences, they can bridge different religious traditions.

Metaphor in Spiritual Texts: Windows to the Transcendent

Religious and spiritual texts across cultures are replete with metaphors that attempt to convey profound truths. These metaphors often address common themes such as the nature of the divine, the human condition, and the path to spiritual fulfillment.

Metaphors for the Divine

1. Light

- Christianity: Jesus is referred to as the "Light of the World" (John 8:12), symbolizing guidance, truth, and the dispelling of darkness (ignorance or sin).
- Islam: The "Light Verse" in the Qur'an (24:35) describes Allah as the "Light of the heavens and the earth," using the metaphor of a lamp within a niche to represent divine guidance.
- Hinduism: The Gayatri Mantra invokes the "radiance of the sun" as a metaphor for divine enlightenment.
- Interpretation: Light symbolizes clarity, purity, and the presence of the divine illuminating the path for believers.

2. Water
    - Buddhism: The mind is often compared to water—when calm, it reflects reality clearly; when disturbed, it becomes murky.
    - Christianity: Water represents purification and rebirth, as in baptism, symbolizing the washing away of sin and the beginning of new life.

- Taoism: The Tao Te Ching praises water for its softness and flexibility, yet its ability to overcome hardness, symbolizing the Tao's subtle power.
- Interpretation: Water embodies concepts of life, cleansing, adaptability, and the flow of existence.

3. Journey or Path
    - Islam: The "Straight Path" (Al-Sirat al-Mustaqim) refers to the way of righteousness and obedience to God's will.
    - Buddhism: The Eightfold Path outlines steps toward enlightenment.
    - Christianity: The metaphor of the "narrow path" leading to life (Matthew 7:14).
    - Interpretation: Life as a journey or path underscores the progressive nature of spiritual development and the choices that lead toward or away from the ultimate goal.

Metaphors for the Human-Divine Relationship

1. Parent and Child

- Christianity: God is frequently referred to as the Father, and believers as His children, emphasizing care, guidance, and love.
- Hinduism: The Upanishads describe the soul's relationship to Brahman as a spark from a fire, implying both sameness and dependence.
- Interpretation: This metaphor conveys intimacy, nurturance, and the inherent connection between the divine and humanity.

2. Lover and Beloved
    - Sufism (Islamic Mysticism): Poets like Rumi use romantic imagery to describe the soul's longing for union with the divine.
    - Bhakti Movement (Hinduism): Devotees express deep love and devotion to deities like Krishna, often using the language of romance.
    - Song of Songs (Judaism and Christianity): An allegorical interpretation of the passionate love between God and His people.
    - Interpretation: Romantic metaphors highlight the intense, personal, and transformative nature of spiritual devotion.

3. Shepherd and Sheep

- Judaism and Christianity: God or spiritual leaders are depicted as shepherds guiding and protecting their flock (e.g., Psalm 23).
- Interpretation: This metaphor emphasizes guidance, protection, and the dependence of followers on divine leadership.

Universal Metaphors Across Traditions

Despite cultural and theological differences, many metaphors recur across religions, pointing to shared human experiences and spiritual insights.

The Tree

- Norse Mythology: Yggdrasil, the World Tree, connects the nine worlds, symbolizing the interconnectedness of all existence.
- Buddhism: The Bodhi Tree under which Siddhartha Gautama attained enlightenment represents wisdom and awakening.
- Christianity: The Tree of Life in Genesis and Revelation symbolizes eternal life and God's provision.

- Interpretation: The tree often symbolizes life, growth, interconnectedness, and the axis between the earthly and the divine.

Fire

- Hinduism: Agni, the fire god, serves as a mediator between humans and gods, representing purification and transformation.
- Christianity: The Holy Spirit is associated with tongues of fire at Pentecost, symbolizing inspiration and divine presence.
- Zoroastrianism: Fire temples use eternal flames as symbols of purity and the divine light.
- Interpretation: Fire represents purification, transformation, and the presence of the sacred.

Metaphor as a Bridge to Universal Truths

Metaphors in spiritual texts function as bridges in several ways:

1. Expressing the Ineffable
    - Metaphors allow for the expression of concepts that are beyond literal description.

The divine, being infinite and transcendent, cannot be fully captured by human language.
    - Example: Describing God as a "rock" conveys stability and strength without implying that God is literally a stone.
2. Connecting Diverse Traditions
    - Shared metaphors highlight commonalities between different religions, fostering understanding and dialogue.
    - Example: The metaphor of light as divine guidance appears in multiple traditions, suggesting a universal recognition of enlightenment.
3. Engaging the Imagination and Emotions
    - Metaphors resonate emotionally and imaginatively, making abstract ideas accessible and meaningful.
    - Example: The lover and beloved metaphor evokes deep emotional connections, illustrating the intensity of spiritual devotion.
4. Facilitating Personal Interpretation

- Metaphors invite individuals to explore and interpret spiritual truths in ways that are personally relevant.
- Example: A "journey" can represent various aspects of spiritual growth unique to each person's experience.

Philosophical Perspectives on Metaphor in Religion

Ludwig Wittgenstein and Language Games

- Wittgenstein suggested that the meaning of words is derived from their use within specific "language games" or contexts.
- In religious contexts, language operates differently than in scientific or everyday discourse.
- Implication: Religious metaphors are part of a language game that conveys meaning within the framework of faith practices.

Metaphor as Cognitive Tool

- Cognitive linguists like George Lakoff and Mark Johnson argue that metaphors are fundamental to human thought.

- Metaphors structure how we perceive and interact with the world, not just literary devices.
- Application to Religion: Metaphorical language shapes religious experiences and understandings.

Symbolic Interactionism

- This sociological perspective emphasizes the creation of meaning through social interactions using symbols.
- Religious metaphors are part of a shared symbolic system that fosters communal identity and understanding.

Challenges and Misinterpretations

While metaphors enrich religious language, they also present challenges:

1. Literalism
    - Taking metaphors literally can lead to misunderstandings or rigid interpretations.
    - Example: Viewing metaphorical descriptions of the divine as literal facts may limit the infinite nature of the divine.

2. Cultural Context
   - Metaphors are often rooted in specific cultural experiences and may not translate directly across cultures.
   - Solution: Engaging in interfaith dialogue to understand the underlying meanings.
3. Idolatry of Language
   - Focusing on the symbols themselves rather than the realities they point to can result in idolatry.
   - Tillich's Warning: Confusing the symbol with the ultimate concern distracts from the true object of faith.

Metaphors in Practice: A Comparative Exploration

Case Study 1: The Heart as a Spiritual Center

- Christianity: The heart is seen as the seat of emotions and faith. "Blessed are the pure in heart" (Matthew 5:8).
- Sufism: The heart is the place where God manifests. Sufis engage in practices to polish the heart's mirror.

- Buddhism: The heart-mind (citta) is central to experiencing reality and cultivating compassion.
- Interpretation: The metaphor of the heart represents the core of one's being where the divine or ultimate reality is encountered.

Case Study 2: Crossing the Ocean

- Hinduism: The ocean symbolizes Samsara, the cycle of birth and rebirth. Spiritual practices are the boat to cross over to liberation.
- Buddhism: Crossing the river/ocean represents moving from ignorance to enlightenment.
- Christianity: Baptism involves water, symbolizing death to the old self and rebirth into new life.
- Interpretation: Water bodies represent barriers or transitions, and crossing them symbolizes transformation and salvation.

Embracing Metaphor for Deeper Understanding

Recognizing the metaphorical nature of religious language opens avenues for deeper spiritual exploration:

1. Encourages Humility

- Acknowledging that language is limited fosters humility in our assertions about the divine.
- Quote: "The Tao that can be told is not the eternal Tao." (Tao Te Ching)

2. Promotes Inclusivity
    - Understanding metaphors as symbolic allows for appreciation of diverse expressions of spirituality.
    - Example: Seeing different religious metaphors as various lenses focusing on the same ultimate reality.
3. Enhances Personal Spirituality
    - Engaging with metaphors enriches personal reflection and can lead to transformative insights.
    - Practice: Meditating on metaphoric passages to uncover layers of meaning.

Conclusion: Metaphor as a Universal Language of the Sacred

Metaphors serve as bridges connecting the finite human experience with the infinite divine reality. They enable us to express the inexpressible, share profound truths across cultural and religious boundaries, and tap into the universal aspects of the human condition.

By embracing the symbolic nature of religious language, we:

- Foster Interfaith Understanding: Recognize that different traditions may use varied metaphors to point toward the same ultimate concerns.
- Deepen Spiritual Insight: Allow metaphors to guide us into deeper contemplation of the mysteries of existence.
- Cultivate Unity: Appreciate the shared human endeavor to seek meaning, purpose, and connection with the greater whole.

In a world marked by diversity of belief, metaphors in spiritual texts remind us that while our languages and symbols may differ, the ultimate realities we seek to understand are shared. They invite us to look beyond the literal and enter into a dialogue that transcends words, touching the very essence of what it means to be human in relation to the divine.

Quotes to Ponder

- **Paul Tillich**: "The language of faith is the language of symbols."
- **Rumi**: "The lamps are different, but the Light is the same."
- **Albert Einstein**: "All religions, arts, and sciences are branches of the same tree."

Final Thoughts

Metaphor is not merely a literary device but a fundamental aspect of how we conceptualize and communicate profound truths. In spirituality, metaphors serve as vital tools that bridge the gap between the known and the unknown, the seen and the unseen. They allow us to share experiences of the sacred in ways that are both deeply personal and universally accessible.

By appreciating the metaphoric language of spiritual texts, we open ourselves to a richer, more nuanced understanding of the divine and our place within the cosmos. We recognize that beneath the diversity of religious expressions lies a common human quest—a journey toward understanding

Chapter 3: Metaphor and Meaning

Section 3.1: The Language of Metaphor

Introduction: The Metaphorical Fabric of Human Language

Language is more than a mere conduit for conveying information; it is a dynamic, living system that shapes and is shaped by human thought and culture. At its core, language is inherently metaphorical. We use metaphors and symbols not only to embellish our speech but to structure our understanding of abstract concepts that are otherwise difficult to grasp. This is particularly evident when we attempt to discuss profound and intangible subjects such as spirituality, existence, and the nature of the divine. Metaphor serves as a bridge between the known and the unknown, the tangible and the intangible, allowing us to navigate complex ideas by relating them to familiar experiences.

In this section, we delve deeper into the metaphorical nature of language and its pivotal role in shaping our comprehension of abstract concepts. We will explore the philosophies of Friedrich Nietzsche and Ludwig Wittgenstein, who critically examined the capacities and limitations of language in expressing truth and meaning. Their insights reveal how our linguistic frameworks influence our perceptions of reality and the divine, and how metaphors are instrumental in this process.

The Ubiquity of Metaphor in Language

Understanding Metaphor: Beyond Literary Devices

A metaphor is traditionally defined as a figure of speech in which a word or phrase is applied to an object or action to which it is not literally applicable, highlighting a resemblance between two different things. However, metaphors are not confined to poetry or rhetoric; they are fundamental to human cognition and communication. We rely on metaphoric structures to conceptualize and articulate our experiences, thoughts, and feelings.

Cognitive Metaphor Theory, developed by linguists George Lakoff and Mark Johnson, posits that our conceptual system is largely metaphorical. According to this theory:

- Conceptual Metaphors: We understand and experience one kind of thing in terms of another. For example, we conceptualize time as money ("spending time," "wasting time," "investing time").
- Embodied Experience: Our metaphors are grounded in physical and sensory experiences, which form the basis for understanding more abstract concepts.

Metaphors Structuring Thought

Metaphors influence not just how we talk but how we think:

- Framing Perceptions: The metaphors we use frame our perceptions of reality. For example, referring to argument as war ("He shot down my argument") frames discussions as combative rather than collaborative.
- Guiding Actions: Metaphoric concepts can guide behavior. If we see life as a journey, we may be more goal-oriented and focused on progress.
- Shaping Values: Metaphors can reflect and reinforce cultural values and beliefs.

Nietzsche's Exploration of Language and Metaphor

Nietzsche's Critique of Language and Truth

Friedrich Nietzsche, a seminal figure in Western philosophy, critically examined the nature of truth, knowledge, and language. In his essay "On Truth and Lies in a Nonmoral Sense" (1873), Nietzsche offers a provocative critique of the conventional understanding of truth:

- Truth as a Metaphor: Nietzsche asserts that what we call "truth" is a collection of metaphors, metonyms, and anthropomorphisms that have been poetically and rhetorically intensified, transferred, and embellished over time.
- The Illusion of Objectivity: He challenges the notion that language can provide an objective representation of reality, arguing that words are arbitrary designations that do not capture the essence of things.
- The Forgetfulness of Metaphor: Over time, metaphors become so ingrained in language that we forget their metaphorical origin, mistaking them for literal truth.

The Formation of Concepts

Nietzsche delves into how concepts are formed through language:

- **Abstraction and Generalization**: Concepts arise from the equation of unequal things. For instance, the concept of a "leaf" is an abstraction that overlooks the individual differences of each leaf.
- **Loss of Uniqueness**: By creating concepts, we strip away the unique characteristics of individual phenomena, reducing them to generalized categories.
- **Language as a Simplification**: Language simplifies the complexity of reality, which can lead to a distorted understanding.

Implications for Understanding the Divine

Nietzsche's insights have profound implications for theology and spirituality:

- **Inaccessibility of Ultimate Reality**: If language cannot capture the true essence of even mundane objects, it is even less capable of conveying the nature of the divine.

- **Constructed Notions of God**: Our ideas about God are shaped by cultural, historical, and linguistic constructs, rather than direct knowledge.
- **Skepticism Toward Metaphysical Claims**: Nietzsche encourages skepticism toward claims of absolute truth, particularly those that rely on language to express transcendent realities.

The Role of Metaphor in Spiritual Discourse

- **Creative Exploration**: Nietzsche suggests that embracing the metaphorical nature of language can lead to creative and novel ways of understanding spirituality.
- **Overcoming Dogmatism**: Recognizing the limitations of language can help overcome rigid dogmas that are based on literal interpretations of metaphoric language.
- **Embracing the Unknowable**: By accepting that the divine may be beyond linguistic expression, individuals can approach spirituality with humility and openness.

Early Wittgenstein: The Picture Theory

In his early work, particularly the **"Tractatus Logico-Philosophicus"** (1921), **Ludwig Wittgenstein** proposes the **Picture Theory of Language**:

- **Language as Representation**: Language functions by mirroring or picturing states of affairs in the world. Words correspond to objects, and sentences correspond to facts.
- **Limits of Language**: Wittgenstein acknowledges that language has limits. He famously concludes the Tractatus with, "Whereof one cannot speak, thereof one must be silent," suggesting that some aspects of reality are beyond linguistic expression.
- **The Ineffable**: Matters such as ethics, aesthetics, and the mystical lie outside the bounds of what can be meaningfully discussed using language.

Later Wittgenstein: Language Games and Forms of Life

In his later work, particularly "Philosophical Investigations" (published posthumously in 1953), Wittgenstein revises his earlier views:

- **Language as Activity**: Language is not a static system of representation but an active part of human life.
- **Language Games**: Wittgenstein introduces the concept of language games, emphasizing that words gain meaning through their use in specific contexts and activities.
- **Forms of Life**: Language is intertwined with the cultural and social practices (forms of life) of a community.
- **Meaning as Use**: The meaning of a word is determined by how it is used within a particular language game.

Understanding the Divine Through Language Games

Applying Wittgenstein's ideas to religious language:

- **Contextual Meaning**: Religious language gains meaning within the context of religious practices and forms of life.
- **Diversity of Language Games**: Different religious traditions engage in different language games, which can lead to varied understandings of similar concepts.

- **Incommensurability**: Attempts to compare or translate religious concepts across different traditions may be challenging due to differing language games.

Mysticism and the Limits of Language

- **Acknowledging the Ineffable**: Wittgenstein's recognition of the limits of language aligns with mystical traditions that emphasize direct, ineffable experiences of the divine.
- **Silence as Expression**: In some cases, silence or non-verbal expression may be more appropriate for conveying spiritual truths that elude language.

Language Shaping Perception of Reality and the Divine

Metaphor in Conceptualizing Abstract Ideas

Metaphors are crucial in conceptualizing abstract ideas:

- **Time as Space**: We often use spatial metaphors to describe time (e.g., "looking forward to the future," "behind schedule").

- **Emotions as Forces**: Emotions are described as external forces acting upon us ("overcome with joy," "struck by sadness").
- **Mind as Container**: Thoughts and ideas are conceptualized as objects within a container ("in my mind," "filled with ideas").

Cultural Influence on Metaphoric Language

Culture plays a significant role in shaping metaphoric language:

- **Collectivist vs. Individualist Societies**: Metaphors in collectivist cultures may emphasize interconnectedness ("the nail that sticks out gets hammered down"), while individualist cultures may emphasize independence ("forge your own path").
- **Religious Metaphors**: Metaphors for the divine vary across cultures, reflecting different values and experiences.

Metaphors Influencing Spiritual Experiences

The metaphors we use can shape our spiritual experiences:

- **Expectation and Interpretation**: If we conceptualize spiritual growth as a journey, we may be more attuned to milestones and progress.
- **Emotional Resonance**: Metaphors that resonate emotionally can deepen our connection to spiritual practices.
- **Limitations**: Relying on certain metaphors may limit our perception, potentially excluding alternative experiences or understandings.

Expanding the Discussion: Additional Philosophical Perspectives

Martin Heidegger: Language as the House of Being

Martin Heidegger (1889–1976), a German philosopher, emphasized the fundamental role of language in shaping human existence:

- **Language Revealing Being**: Heidegger posited that language is not merely a tool but the medium through which Being is disclosed.

- **Poetic Language**: He highlighted the importance of poetry and metaphor in revealing truths that lie beyond literal expression.
- **The Limitations of Technical Language**: Heidegger critiqued the dominance of technical and scientific language, which he believed could obscure deeper existential truths.

Jacques Derrida: Deconstruction and the Play of Language

Jacques Derrida (1930–2004), a French philosopher, introduced the concept of **deconstruction**, examining the instability of meaning in language:

- **Différance**: Derrida coined the term "différance" to illustrate how meaning is always deferred, and words gain meaning through their differences from other words.
- **Metaphors as Unstable**: He argued that metaphors are inherently unstable and can subvert the very concepts they are meant to convey.
- **Implications for Theology**: Derrida's ideas suggest that theological concepts are open to endless reinterpretation and that language can never fully capture the divine.

Cognitive Science and Embodied Metaphor

Modern cognitive science supports the centrality of metaphor in human thought:

- **Embodied Cognition**: Our understanding is grounded in bodily experiences.
- **Neuroscience of Metaphor**: Studies show that metaphoric language activates sensory and motor areas of the brain associated with the literal meanings of words.
- **Implications for Spirituality**: Understanding the neural basis of metaphor can shed light on how spiritual experiences are processed and expressed.

Final Thoughts

The language of metaphor is not just a tool for embellishment but a fundamental aspect of human cognition and communication. It allows us to grapple with the abstract and the ineffable, providing a bridge between our tangible experiences and the profound mysteries of existence. By engaging thoughtfully with metaphoric language, we can enrich our understanding, foster deeper connections with others, and perhaps come closer to glimpsing the realities that lie beyond the reach of words.

Section 3.2: God as a Metaphor

The concept of God has been a cornerstone of human thought and spirituality for millennia. Across cultures and epochs, people have grappled with the idea of the divine, seeking to understand the mysteries of existence and the universe. Yet, despite—or perhaps because of—its centrality, the nature of God often eludes precise definition. The divine is frequently described as ineffable, transcending human comprehension and language. To bridge this vast chasm between the finite human mind and the infinite divine, we turn to metaphor.

Metaphor serves as a vital tool in our quest to articulate the inexpressible. By relating the unknown to the known, metaphors allow us to approach complex and abstract concepts through more familiar terms. In the realm of spirituality, viewing God as a metaphor for the universal source offers a way to conceptualize the divine in a manner that is both accessible and profound.

Consider the way various religious traditions employ metaphor to convey their understanding of the divine. In Hinduism, the concept of Brahman represents the ultimate reality—the unchanging, infinite source of all that exists. Brahman is often likened to an ocean, with individual souls (Atman) compared to drops of water. Just as drops are part of the ocean, so too are individual souls part of the universal source. This metaphor emphasizes unity and interconnectedness, illustrating how the divine permeates all aspects of existence.

Similarly, Taoism speaks of the Tao, or "The Way," as the underlying natural order of the universe. The Tao is ineffable and cannot be fully captured in words. As the Tao Te Ching poetically states, "The Tao that can be told is not the eternal Tao." Metaphors such as water flowing effortlessly around obstacles or the uncarved block symbolize the Tao's subtle yet all-encompassing presence. These images invite practitioners to align themselves with the natural flow of the universe, embracing simplicity and harmony.

In Buddhism, particularly within the Mahayana tradition, the concept of the Dharmakaya—the "truth body"—represents the ultimate nature of reality. It is beyond form and defies direct description, often approached through metaphoric expressions. The Dharmakaya is likened to space: boundless, pervasive, and encompassing all phenomena without being altered by them. This metaphor helps convey the idea of an ultimate reality that is ever-present yet transcendent of individual distinctions.

These examples illustrate how metaphors enable us to engage with the divine by drawing parallels with more tangible experiences. They serve as bridges between the human and the transcendent, allowing us to explore spiritual truths that might otherwise remain inaccessible.

One philosopher who profoundly embraced the idea of God as a metaphor for the universal source was Baruch Spinoza. Living in the 17th century, a time of significant scientific and philosophical development, Spinoza challenged traditional notions of God and religion. In his magnum opus, *Ethics*, he presents a vision of the divine that is both radical and deeply insightful.

Spinoza's philosophy is rooted in pantheism, the belief that God and the universe are one and the same. For Spinoza, there is only one substance in the universe, which he identifies as God or Nature (*Deus sive Natura*). This singular substance possesses infinite attributes, and everything that exists is a mode—an expression—of this substance. In other words, all individual things are manifestations of the one universal reality.

By equating God with the universe, Spinoza offers a metaphor that elevates the natural world to divine status. The cosmos itself becomes a sacred entity, imbued with the essence of the divine. This perspective dissolves the boundary between creator and creation, emphasizing the immanence of God—that the divine is fully present within the world rather than existing as a separate, transcendent being.

Spinoza's pantheism carries profound ethical implications. If everything is a manifestation of the divine, then understanding the natural laws and the inherent order of the universe becomes a spiritual endeavor. Knowledge of the world leads to knowledge of God. This realization fosters a sense of unity and harmony with all that exists, encouraging individuals to live in accordance with the rational, natural order.

However, Spinoza's ideas were controversial in his time. His rejection of a personal, anthropomorphic God and his identification of God with Nature led to accusations of atheism. Yet, rather than denying the divine, Spinoza sought to redefine it in a way that was consistent with reason and the emerging scientific understanding of his era. By viewing God as the universal source—the totality of existence—he provided a metaphor that transcended traditional religious doctrines and invited a new way of relating to the divine.

In contemporary thought, the metaphor of God as the universal source continues to resonate. Process theology, for example, views God not as a static, unchanging being but as a dynamic process involved in the unfolding of the universe. This perspective aligns with Spinoza's emphasis on the immanence of the divine and the interconnectedness of all things.

Similarly, panentheism—the belief that the universe is part of God, but God also transcends the universe—utilizes metaphor to express the complex relationship between the divine and the cosmos. This viewpoint maintains that while God includes all that exists, there is still an aspect of the divine that goes beyond the material world. Metaphor becomes essential in conveying this nuanced understanding, as it allows for the expression of both immanence and transcendence.

Even within scientific discourse, metaphoric conceptions of God emerge. Albert Einstein, inspired by Spinoza, spoke of a "cosmic religion" grounded in the awe and wonder of the universe's harmony. For Einstein, God was synonymous with the order and rationality inherent in the natural laws governing the cosmos. This metaphorical interpretation bridges the gap between science and spirituality, suggesting that the pursuit of scientific knowledge can be a pathway to experiencing the divine.

Embracing God as a metaphor for the universal source carries significant implications for personal spirituality and ethical living. It encourages individuals to look beyond anthropomorphic depictions of the divine and to recognize the sacredness inherent in the natural world and in themselves. This perspective fosters a deep sense of connection and responsibility toward all forms of life and the environment.

Moreover, viewing God metaphorically can facilitate interfaith dialogue and understanding. By acknowledging that different religions employ various metaphors to articulate similar fundamental truths, we can appreciate the diversity of spiritual expression while recognizing our shared human quest for meaning and connection.

However, it's important to consider potential critiques of this approach. Some may argue that interpreting God solely as a metaphor risks diminishing the divine's reality or undermining traditional beliefs in a personal deity. For individuals who find comfort and guidance in a personal relationship with God, a metaphorical interpretation might seem insufficient or impersonal.

Additionally, there is a risk of reductionism—oversimplifying complex theological concepts or dismissing the depth of religious traditions. To mitigate these concerns, it's crucial to approach the metaphor of God as an invitation to deeper exploration rather than a definitive conclusion. Metaphor serves not to confine our understanding but to expand it, allowing room for mystery, wonder, and continual discovery.

In practice, integrating the metaphor of God as the universal source into one's spiritual life can take many forms. Contemplative practices such as meditation and mindfulness can help individuals experience a sense of unity with the cosmos. Artistic expression—through music, visual arts, or literature—provides avenues for exploring and communicating one's relationship with the divine in personal and creative ways.

Engaging in community rituals and participating in shared symbolic actions can reinforce a collective sense of connection to the universal source. Such practices emphasize the importance of relationships—not only among people but also between humanity and the natural world.

Ultimately, viewing God as a metaphor for the universal source enriches our understanding of spirituality by highlighting the interconnectedness of all things. It challenges us to transcend limited conceptions and to embrace a more expansive vision of the divine—one that encompasses the entirety of existence. This perspective invites us to consider that perhaps the divine is not something external to be sought after but is inherent within us and the world around us.

As we navigate the complexities of modern life, the metaphor of God as the universal source offers a unifying principle that can inspire ethical living, environmental stewardship, and a deeper sense of purpose. It encourages us to cultivate compassion, empathy, and a recognition of our shared humanity. In a world often divided by differences, this metaphor serves as a reminder of the profound connections that bind us all.

Through the lens of metaphor, we can approach the divine not as a distant, incomprehensible entity but as an ever-present reality that permeates every aspect of our lives. This understanding resonates with the teachings of many spiritual traditions and thinkers who have sought to articulate the inexpressible. By embracing metaphor, we open ourselves to a richer, more nuanced relationship with the divine—a relationship that transcends words and touches the very essence of our being.

Section 3.3: The Role of Symbols in Spiritual Practices

Symbols have been integral to human spirituality since the dawn of consciousness. Across cultures and religions, symbols serve as bridges between the tangible and the intangible, the known and the mysterious. They encapsulate complex spiritual truths in simple, recognizable forms, allowing individuals to connect with profound ideas through sensory experience. Symbols like the cross, the crescent moon, and the lotus flower are not merely decorative or cultural artifacts; they are profound representations of deeper spiritual realities. These symbols point beyond themselves to a universal source, a unifying truth that transcends individual traditions and unites humanity in a shared quest for meaning.

Understanding the Power of Symbols

At their core, symbols are multivalent—they carry multiple layers of meaning that can be interpreted in various ways depending on the context and the individual's perspective. This richness allows symbols to communicate complex ideas succinctly and powerfully. They operate on both conscious and subconscious levels, tapping into archetypal images and shared human experiences.

Symbols function in spiritual practices in several key ways:

1. Facilitating Connection with the Divine: Symbols provide a focal point for meditation, prayer, and worship, helping individuals concentrate their thoughts and open themselves to spiritual experiences.

2. Conveying Spiritual Teachings: They encapsulate doctrines and philosophies in visual or tangible forms, making abstract concepts more accessible.
3. Creating a Sense of Community: Shared symbols foster a collective identity among practitioners, uniting them through common beliefs and rituals.
4. Serving as Tools for Transformation: Engaging with symbols can inspire personal growth, self-reflection, and a deeper understanding of one's place in the universe.

Importantly, symbols are not ends in themselves. Their true significance lies in their ability to point beyond the literal to the metaphysical. By recognizing symbols as gateways rather than destinations, individuals can move beyond surface interpretations to explore the deeper spiritual truths they represent.

The Cross: A Symbol of Sacrifice and Redemption

In Christianity, the cross stands as the preeminent symbol, rich with historical and theological significance. Originally an instrument of execution in the Roman Empire, the cross was transformed into a symbol of hope, salvation, and eternal life.

- Historical Context: According to Christian belief, Jesus of Nazareth was crucified on a cross, an event that is central to the faith's narrative of redemption.
- Spiritual Significance:
  - Sacrifice: The cross represents the ultimate sacrifice—Jesus giving his life for the salvation of humanity.
  - Redemption: It symbolizes the possibility of forgiveness and reconciliation with God.
  - Resurrection: The empty cross also signifies the resurrection, embodying the victory over death and the promise of eternal life.
- Universal Themes:
  - Love and Compassion: The cross is a reminder of selfless love and the call to love others unconditionally.
  - Suffering and Hope: It acknowledges the reality of suffering while offering hope for transformation and renewal.

For believers, the cross serves as a visual shorthand for the entirety of Christian doctrine, encapsulating complex theological concepts in a simple form. It is a pointer to the divine mystery of God's love and the interconnectedness of all people through that love.

The Crescent Moon: A Symbol of Guidance and Renewal

In Islam, the crescent moon holds significant symbolic value, often seen atop mosques and in Islamic art. While not originally an Islamic symbol, it has come to represent the faith in the modern world.

- Historical Development:
    - The crescent moon and star became associated with Islam during the Ottoman Empire, which adopted it as a symbol of sovereignty.
    - Over time, it gained broader acceptance as a symbol representing Islamic identity.
- Spiritual Significance:
    - Guidance: The moon provides light in the darkness, symbolizing guidance and the illumination provided by faith.
    - Renewal: The lunar cycle represents the cyclical nature of time and the opportunity for continual renewal and repentance.
    - Connection to Rituals: The Islamic calendar is lunar-based, with important events like

Ramadan determined by the phases of the moon.

- Universal Themes:
    - Reflection and Contemplation: The moon's gentle light invites introspection and spiritual contemplation.
    - Harmony with Nature: Emphasizes the importance of aligning one's life with the natural rhythms of the universe.

The crescent moon serves as a metaphoric link between the celestial and the terrestrial, reminding believers of the greater cosmos and their place within it. It points toward the divine order and the guidance that comes from aligning oneself with that order.

The Lotus Flower: A Symbol of Purity and Enlightenment

In Buddhism and Hinduism, the lotus flower is a powerful symbol of spiritual awakening and purity.

- Natural Characteristics:
    - The lotus grows in muddy waters but rises above the surface to bloom in pristine beauty.
    - It closes at night and opens with the first light of dawn, symbolizing renewal.

- Spiritual Significance:
  - Purity: Represents the purity of the soul and the potential to rise above earthly impurities.
  - Enlightenment: Symbolizes the journey toward enlightenment and the blossoming of spiritual understanding.
  - Detachment: The lotus remains unstained by the mud it grows in, reflecting the ideal of remaining detached from worldly desires.
- Association with Deities:
  - In Hinduism, gods and goddesses like Lakshmi and Brahma are often depicted seated on lotus flowers, signifying their divine nature.
  - In Buddhism, the Buddha is frequently shown sitting on a lotus throne, representing his enlightened state.
- Universal Themes:
  - Resilience and Growth: The lotus embodies the ability to overcome obstacles and emerge stronger.

- Inner Beauty: Highlights the importance of inner purity and the beauty that comes from spiritual development.

The lotus flower is a living metaphor for the spiritual journey, illustrating how individuals can transcend their circumstances to achieve higher states of consciousness. It points to the universal potential for growth and transformation inherent in all beings.

Other Symbols Across Traditions

Symbols are abundant across various spiritual traditions, each pointing toward deeper truths:

- The Wheel of Dharma (Buddhism): Represents the teachings of the Buddha and the path to enlightenment. The wheel's continuous circle signifies the cycle of birth, death, and rebirth, while its spokes symbolize the Noble Eightfold Path.
- The Star of David (Judaism): Consists of two interlocking triangles, symbolizing the connection between God and humanity. It reflects the interplay of the divine and the earthly, the spiritual and the physical.

- The Om (Hinduism): A sacred sound and symbol representing the ultimate reality, consciousness, or Atman. It embodies the essence of the universe and the interconnectedness of all existence.
- The Ankh (Ancient Egypt): A cross with a loop at the top, symbolizing eternal life and the union of male and female principles. It represents the life-giving power and the continuity of existence.
- The Yin Yang (Taoism): Illustrates the concept of duality and balance—how seemingly opposite forces are interconnected and interdependent. It emphasizes harmony and the dynamic equilibrium of the universe.

Each of these symbols, while rooted in specific cultural and religious contexts, points beyond itself to universal principles. They convey messages about the nature of reality, the human condition, and the path to spiritual fulfillment.

Symbols as Pointers to the Universal Source

The common thread among these diverse symbols is their role as pointers to something greater—a universal source or ultimate reality that transcends individual differences. They function as tools that help individuals:

- Connect with the Transcendent: By engaging with symbols, practitioners can experience a sense of connection with the divine or the ultimate truth.
- Access Inner Wisdom: Symbols often resonate on a subconscious level, tapping into archetypal images and facilitating personal insight.
- Cultivate Unity: Recognizing that symbols across traditions point to similar truths can foster a sense of unity and shared humanity.

Consider the mandala in Buddhism and Hinduism—a geometric configuration of symbols that represents the universe. Mandalas are used as instruments of meditation, guiding individuals toward a state of wholeness and integration. The intricate patterns draw the mind inward, encouraging contemplation of the cosmos and one's place within it. Similarly, in Christian traditions, the use of icons and sacred art serves as a window to the divine, inviting reflection and veneration.

Symbols also play a crucial role in rituals and ceremonies, providing structure and meaning to communal practices.

They mark significant moments in the life cycle—birth, initiation, marriage, death—and seasonal festivals, grounding these events in a larger spiritual context.

The Transformative Power of Symbols

Engaging with spiritual symbols can have profound effects on individuals:

- Emotional Impact: Symbols can evoke deep feelings, from awe and reverence to comfort and inspiration. This emotional resonance can strengthen faith and motivate ethical action.
- Psychological Integration: By embodying complex ideas, symbols can help individuals integrate different aspects of themselves, promoting psychological wholeness.
- Guidance and Support: Symbols can serve as anchors during times of uncertainty, providing guidance and a sense of stability.
- Catalysts for Change: They can inspire transformation by challenging individuals to reflect on their beliefs and behaviors.

For example, the practice of wearing a cross or carrying a rosary in Christianity serves as a constant reminder of one's faith and values. In Islam, the act of prayer five times a day, often oriented toward the Kaaba in Mecca—a symbol of unity and direction—reinforces discipline and mindfulness.

Interpreting Symbols in a Modern Context

In the contemporary world, symbols continue to evolve and take on new meanings. Globalization and interfaith interactions have led to increased exposure to diverse symbols, fostering greater understanding but also potential misunderstandings.

- Cultural Sensitivity: It's important to approach symbols with respect for their origins and significance within their traditions.
- Personal Interpretation: Individuals may find personal meaning in symbols outside their original context, using them as tools for personal growth.
- Artistic Expression: Symbols are frequently incorporated into art, literature, and media, reflecting and shaping societal values.

However, there is a risk of symbolic dilution when symbols are commercialized or detached from their deeper meanings. To maintain their transformative power, it's essential to engage with symbols thoughtfully and intentionally.

Symbols as Bridges Between Traditions

Recognizing that many symbols share common themes can foster interfaith dialogue and mutual respect. For instance:

- Light: Symbolizes knowledge, purity, and the divine in many traditions. The use of candles in religious ceremonies across faiths highlights this shared symbolism.
- Trees: Represent life, growth, and connection between heaven and earth. The Tree of Life appears in Christianity, Judaism, Islam, and Norse mythology.
- Water: Symbolizes purification, renewal, and life. Rituals involving water, such as baptism in Christianity and ablutions in Islam, underscore its universal significance.

By acknowledging these shared symbols, individuals and communities can appreciate the common ground between different spiritual paths, promoting peace and understanding.

Moving Beyond Symbols to Direct Experience

While symbols are invaluable tools, spiritual traditions often emphasize the importance of moving beyond symbols to direct experience:

- Transcending the Symbol: Recognizing that symbols are maps, not the territory. They point the way but are not the destination.
- Inner Realization: Encouraging practitioners to seek personal encounters with the divine or ultimate reality, beyond conceptual representations.
- Mystical Traditions: In many mystical paths, such as Sufism in Islam or Zen in Buddhism, there is an emphasis on direct, unmediated experience of the sacred.

As Laozi writes in the Tao Te Ching: "The name that can be named is not the eternal name." This suggests that while symbols and names are helpful, they are ultimately insufficient to fully capture the essence of the Tao.

Conclusion: Embracing Symbols as Gateways to Unity

Symbols in spiritual practices are powerful conduits for conveying profound truths. They serve as gateways that lead individuals toward deeper understanding, personal transformation, and connection with the universal source that unites all beings. By engaging with symbols thoughtfully, we can:

- Deepen Our Spiritual Practice: Allowing symbols to guide our meditation, prayer, and contemplation.
- Foster Unity and Compassion: Recognizing the shared symbolism across traditions can cultivate empathy and solidarity.
- Encourage Personal Growth: Using symbols as tools for self-reflection and development.
- Promote Cultural Appreciation: Respecting the origins and meanings of symbols enhances intercultural understanding.

In a world rich with diverse spiritual expressions, symbols offer a common language that transcends words. They remind us that beneath the surface differences lies a shared human quest for meaning, purpose, and connection. By seeing symbols not as ends in themselves but as pointers to the universal source, we honor their true purpose and open ourselves to the profound mysteries they represent.

Chapter 4: From Skeptic to Seeker

Section 4.1: The Journey of Doubt

Doubt is often perceived as an obstacle to faith and spirituality—a barrier that separates us from certainty and peace. However, throughout history, doubt has also been a catalyst for profound personal growth and deeper understanding. Embracing skepticism can lead to a more authentic and robust spirituality, one that is not based on blind acceptance but on thoughtful inquiry and genuine conviction.

In this chapter, we explore how the journey of doubt can transform an individual from a skeptic into a seeker. We delve into the philosophical tradition of **Socratic questioning**, examining how this method of critical inquiry can serve as a model for spiritual exploration. By embracing doubt as a natural and valuable part of the human experience, we can open ourselves to new perspectives, challenge our assumptions, and embark on a path toward deeper truth.

The Nature of Doubt

Doubt arises when we encounter questions that challenge our existing beliefs or when we face experiences that cannot be easily explained within our current frameworks. It can be unsettling, provoking feelings of uncertainty and vulnerability. However, doubt is also a sign of an active, engaged mind—a mind that is not content with superficial answers but seeks to understand the underlying truths of existence.

- **Healthy Skepticism**: Distinguishing between cynicism and constructive skepticism is crucial. While cynicism dismisses possibilities outright, healthy skepticism involves questioning assumptions and seeking evidence.
- **Catalyst for Growth**: Doubt prompts us to re-evaluate our beliefs, leading to personal development and a more nuanced understanding of the world.
- **Universal Experience**: Throughout history, many spiritual seekers and thinkers have grappled with doubt as part of their journeys.

Socrates and the Art of Questioning

One of the most influential figures in the tradition of critical inquiry is **Socrates** (470–399 BCE), the classical Greek philosopher who is considered one of the founders of Western philosophy. Socrates did not leave behind written works; our knowledge of his teachings comes primarily from his student **Plato**. Socrates is renowned for his method of dialogue and questioning, now known as the **Socratic method**.

The Socratic Method

The Socratic method is a form of cooperative argumentative dialogue that stimulates critical thinking and illuminates ideas. It involves asking a series of questions that challenge assumptions and lead the interlocutor to a deeper understanding.

- **Key Features**:
    - **Elenchus**: The technique of refutation, questioning an interlocutor to expose contradictions in their beliefs.
    - **Maieutics**: Derived from the Greek word for midwifery, it refers to the process of helping others bring forth knowledge from within themselves.

- **Dialectic Process**: A dialogue between two or more people holding different points of view, aiming to establish truth through reasoned argumentation.

Applying the Socratic Method to Spiritual Inquiry

- **Questioning Assumptions**: Socratic questioning encourages individuals to examine the foundations of their beliefs. This can lead to a more authentic and personal spirituality, free from unexamined dogma.
- **Embracing Uncertainty**: Acknowledging what we do not know opens the door to learning and growth. Socrates famously stated, "I know that I know nothing," highlighting the importance of intellectual humility.
- **Seeking Definitions**: By exploring the meanings of concepts like justice, virtue, and the good life, Socrates sought to understand the essence of these ideas. Similarly, spiritual seekers can delve into the meanings of faith, enlightenment, or the divine.

Doubt as a Pathway to Deeper Truth

Embracing doubt does not mean abandoning belief; rather, it involves engaging with our beliefs critically and thoughtfully. This process can lead to:

- **Strengthened Convictions**: Through examination, we may find that our beliefs hold up to scrutiny, reinforcing our commitment to them.
- **Refined Beliefs**: We may adjust our beliefs based on new insights, leading to a more nuanced and mature understanding.
- **Expanded Perspectives**: Questioning can open us to new ideas and traditions, enriching our spiritual lives.

Historical Examples of Doubt Leading to Spiritual Growth

1. **St. Augustine of Hippo**:
    - **Background**: Augustine (354–430 CE) was a theologian and philosopher whose writings influenced the development of Western Christianity.
    - **Journey of Doubt**: He grappled with skepticism and explored various philosophies before converting to Christianity.

- **Outcome**: His struggles with doubt led to profound insights about faith, grace, and the human condition, articulated in works like *Confessions*.

2. **The Buddha (Siddhartha Gautama)**:
    - **Background**: Born a prince in ancient India, Siddhartha Gautama renounced his royal life in search of truth.
    - **Journey of Doubt**: He questioned the prevailing religious practices and philosophies of his time.
    - **Outcome**: His doubts propelled him toward deep meditation and ultimately enlightenment, forming the foundation of Buddhism.

3. **René Descartes**:
    - **Background**: A 17th-century French philosopher, mathematician, and scientist.
    - **Journey of Doubt**: Descartes employed methodological skepticism, doubting all beliefs that could be called into question.
    - **Outcome**: He arrived at the foundational statement "Cogito, ergo sum" ("I think,

therefore I am"), establishing a basis for knowledge.

Transforming Doubt into Inquiry

To harness doubt as a tool for spiritual growth, one can adopt several practices inspired by the Socratic method and philosophical inquiry:

1. Cultivate Intellectual Humility

- **Acknowledging Limits**: Recognize the limits of your knowledge and be open to learning.
- **Avoiding Dogmatism**: Resist the temptation to cling rigidly to beliefs without examination.

2. Engage in Reflective Questioning

- **Self-Inquiry**: Regularly reflect on your beliefs and why you hold them.
- **Ask Open-Ended Questions**: Encourage exploration rather than seeking immediate answers.

3. Dialogue with Others

- **Seek Diverse Perspectives**: Engage with people from different backgrounds and traditions.

- **Practice Active Listening**: Truly hear and consider others' viewpoints without rushing to judgment.

4. Embrace Uncertainty

- **Accept Ambiguity**: Recognize that not all questions have clear or definitive answers.
- **Find Comfort in the Journey**: View the search for understanding as an ongoing process.

The Balance Between Doubt and Faith

While doubt can be a powerful catalyst for growth, it is essential to balance skepticism with openness to experience and trust in the process.

- **Constructive Doubt vs. Destructive Doubt**:
  - **Constructive Doubt**: Leads to deeper understanding, fosters curiosity, and encourages exploration.
  - **Destructive Doubt**: Results in cynicism, paralysis, or disengagement from the search for meaning.
- **Faith as a Complement to Doubt**:

- **Dynamic Relationship**: Faith and doubt are not opposites but can coexist, each enriching the other.
- **Faith in the Process**: Trusting that the journey of inquiry will lead to growth, even if the destination is uncertain.

In contemporary spiritual practices, the principles of Socratic questioning can be applied in various ways:

Mindfulness and Meditation

- **Observing Thoughts**: Meditation encourages observing thoughts without judgment, similar to examining beliefs through questioning.
- **Cultivating Awareness**: Increases self-awareness and understanding of one's thought patterns.

Philosophical Counseling

- **Guided Inquiry**: Philosophical counselors use questioning techniques to help clients explore existential concerns.
- **Clarifying Values**: Assists individuals in articulating and aligning with their core values.

Educational Settings

- **Socratic Seminars**: Used in classrooms to foster critical thinking and dialogue.
- **Ethics and Philosophy Courses**: Encourage students to question assumptions and develop reasoning skills.

Challenges and Considerations

While embracing doubt can be transformative, it also presents challenges:

- **Emotional Discomfort**: Confronting deeply held beliefs can be unsettling.
- **Social Pressures**: Communities may resist questioning of established doctrines.
- **Risk of Relativism**: Excessive skepticism can lead to the belief that there is no truth, which may hinder meaningful exploration.

Overcoming Challenges

- **Supportive Communities**: Seek out groups that value inquiry and open dialogue.
- **Personal Resilience**: Develop coping strategies to manage uncertainty and discomfort.

- **Guidance from Mentors**: Engage with teachers or leaders who encourage questioning while providing support.

Embracing the Journey

The journey from skeptic to seeker is deeply personal and unique to each individual. It involves:

- **Self-Discovery**: Gaining insight into one's beliefs, values, and desires.
- **Growth Mindset**: Viewing challenges as opportunities for learning.
- **Authenticity**: Aligning actions and beliefs with one's true self.

By embracing doubt as a natural and valuable part of the spiritual journey, we can move toward a more profound understanding of ourselves and the world. The process of questioning becomes not a barrier to spirituality but a pathway to deeper connection and meaning.

Conclusion

Doubt need not be feared or suppressed; instead, it can be welcomed as a companion on the spiritual path. Like Socrates, we can use questioning to peel back layers of assumption and reach toward deeper truths. This approach transforms skepticism from a force of separation into a bridge that connects us to greater wisdom and understanding.

In the words of the poet Rainer Maria Rilke:

"Be patient toward all that is unsolved in your heart and try to love the questions themselves."

By loving the questions and embracing the journey of doubt, we open ourselves to the richness of the spiritual quest—a journey that leads not only to answers but to a more profound appreciation of the mystery and wonder of existence.

Section 4.2: Personal Transformation Through Inquiry

The journey from doubt to spiritual insight is a profound and deeply personal experience that has been traversed by countless individuals throughout history. This transformation often begins with questioning long-held beliefs and seeking answers to fundamental questions about existence, purpose, and the nature of the universe. By embracing inquiry, individuals open themselves to new perspectives, leading to a broader and more inclusive understanding of spirituality.

In this section, we explore personal stories of transformation that illustrate how questioning can be a catalyst for spiritual awakening. These narratives demonstrate that doubt is not a barrier but a gateway to deeper insight and connection with the universal truths that bind us all.

The Story of Siddhartha Gautama: From Prince to Buddha

Background

Siddhartha Gautama, who would become known as the Buddha, was born around the 6th century BCE in what is now Nepal. Born into a royal family, he lived a life of luxury and was shielded from the suffering of the world by his father, who hoped Siddhartha would become a great king.

Journey of Doubt and Inquiry

- Encounter with Suffering: At the age of 29, Siddhartha ventured outside the palace walls and encountered the "Four Sights"—an old man, a sick person, a dead body, and a wandering ascetic. These

experiences shattered his sheltered worldview and ignited deep questions about the nature of suffering and the impermanence of life.
- Renunciation: Disturbed by these revelations, he renounced his princely life and embarked on a quest to understand the causes of suffering and the path to liberation.
- Ascetic Practices: Siddhartha pursued various spiritual disciplines, including extreme asceticism, but found that they did not provide the answers he sought.
- Meditation and Enlightenment: Ultimately, he resolved to meditate under the Bodhi tree until he attained understanding. After a profound inner struggle, he achieved enlightenment, realizing the Four Noble Truths and the Eightfold Path.

Transformation and Insight

- Founding Buddhism: Siddhartha became the Buddha, "the awakened one," and dedicated his life to teaching others the path to overcoming suffering.
- Inclusive Understanding: His teachings emphasized compassion, mindfulness, and the potential for all

beings to attain enlightenment, transcending social and religious boundaries of his time.

Impact

The Buddha's journey exemplifies how doubt and relentless inquiry can lead to profound spiritual insight. His teachings continue to influence millions worldwide, offering a path to understanding the nature of reality and the mind.

The Transformation of Saint Teresa of Ávila

Background

Teresa Sánchez de Cepeda y Ahumada, known as Teresa of Ávila (1515–1582), was a Spanish nun, mystic, and reformer of the Carmelite Order. Raised in a devout Catholic family, she entered the convent at a young age.

Journey of Doubt and Inquiry

- Spiritual Dryness: For many years, Teresa struggled with spiritual dryness and dissatisfaction with the superficial religious practices she observed.

- Questioning Practices: She began to question the rigor and authenticity of the convent life, feeling that it lacked true devotion and discipline.
- Mystical Experiences: Through deep prayer and contemplation, Teresa experienced profound mystical visions and a sense of intimate union with the divine.

Transformation and Insight

- Reformation Efforts: Motivated by her experiences, she initiated reforms within the Carmelite Order, emphasizing a return to simplicity, poverty, and contemplative prayer.
- Writings: Teresa authored several influential works, including *The Interior Castle* and *The Way of Perfection*, which detailed her spiritual insights and guidance for others seeking deeper connection with God.

Impact

Teresa's journey from doubt to spiritual depth showcases the power of personal inquiry in transforming not only oneself but also broader religious practices. Her emphasis on inner experience and authentic devotion has had a lasting influence on Christian mysticism.

Leo Tolstoy's Search for Meaning

Background

Leo Tolstoy (1828–1910) was a Russian novelist best known for works like *War and Peace* and *Anna Karenina*. Despite his literary success, Tolstoy grappled with existential questions and a deep sense of meaninglessness.

Journey of Doubt and Inquiry

- Crisis of Meaning: In his 50s, Tolstoy experienced a spiritual crisis, questioning the purpose of life and contemplating suicide.
- Exploration of Philosophy and Religion: He delved into philosophical texts, science, and religious teachings but found no satisfactory answers.
- Turning to the Peasantry: Observing the simple faith of Russian peasants, Tolstoy began to see value in a practical, lived spirituality.

Transformation and Insight

- Embracing Simplicity: Tolstoy adopted a lifestyle of simplicity, manual labor, and pacifism.

- Religious and Ethical Writings: He wrote *A Confession*, *The Kingdom of God Is Within You*, and other works articulating his spiritual philosophy, emphasizing non-violence, compassion, and the teachings of Jesus stripped of dogma.

Impact

Tolstoy's journey illustrates how deep questioning can lead to a radical reevaluation of one's life and values. His ideas influenced figures like Mahatma Gandhi and Martin Luther King Jr., contributing to global movements for non-violent resistance.

Malcolm X: From Nation of Islam to Universal Humanism

Background

Malcolm X (1925–1965), born Malcolm Little, was an African American minister and human rights activist who became a prominent figure during the civil rights movement.

Journey of Doubt and Inquiry

- Early Life and Conversion: While in prison, Malcolm converted to the Nation of Islam (NOI), adopting its teachings and changing his surname to "X" to symbolize the loss of his African heritage.
- Rising Influence: As a leader within the NOI, he advocated for black empowerment and separation from white society.
- Growing Doubts: Over time, Malcolm became disillusioned with the NOI's leadership and doctrines, particularly after learning of moral inconsistencies.
- Pilgrimage to Mecca: Seeking truth, he undertook the Hajj pilgrimage to Mecca in 1964.

Transformation and Insight

- Spiritual Awakening: In Mecca, Malcolm experienced a profound sense of unity among people of all races and backgrounds.
- Shift in Perspective: He embraced Sunni Islam and began to advocate for racial unity and human rights on a global scale.
- Establishment of New Organizations: He founded the Muslim Mosque, Inc., and the Organization of Afro-American Unity to promote his new vision.

Impact

Malcolm X's transformation demonstrates how questioning and openness to new experiences can lead to significant shifts in understanding. His legacy continues to inspire discussions on race, identity, and social justice.

Helen Keller's Journey from Darkness to Light

Background

Helen Keller (1880–1968) lost her sight and hearing at 19 months old due to an illness. With the help of her teacher, Anne Sullivan, she learned to communicate and became an author and activist.

Journey of Doubt and Inquiry

- Early Isolation: Keller's inability to communicate led to frustration and isolation.
- Breakthrough with Language: Anne Sullivan taught Keller to understand language through tactile methods, opening a new world of understanding.
- Philosophical and Spiritual Exploration: Keller pursued higher education and became interested in

philosophy and religion, questioning traditional notions due to her unique experiences.

Transformation and Insight

- Embrace of Spiritual Concepts: She developed a personal spirituality that emphasized universal principles of love, hope, and resilience.
- Advocacy: Keller became a prominent advocate for people with disabilities, women's rights, and social justice.

Impact

Keller's life illustrates how overcoming personal challenges through inquiry and education can lead to profound personal growth and the ability to inspire others.

Common Themes in Personal Transformations

These stories, though diverse in context and background, share common elements:

- Catalyst of Doubt: Each individual faced experiences or realizations that disrupted their previous beliefs or understanding.

- Active Inquiry: They engaged in deep questioning, exploration, and openness to new ideas.
- Inner Transformation: The process led to significant changes in their perspectives, values, and ways of life.
- Broader Understanding: Their journeys resulted in more inclusive, compassionate, and universal approaches to spirituality and humanity.
- Impact on Others: Their transformations not only affected their own lives but also inspired and influenced others, contributing to broader social and spiritual movements.

Embracing Personal Inquiry in Your Journey

Drawing inspiration from these narratives, individuals can consider the following steps in their own journeys:

1. Acknowledge Doubt as Natural
   - Understand that questioning is a natural part of growth and does not signify weakness or failure.
2. Seek Knowledge and Experience

- Explore diverse sources of wisdom—books, teachings, conversations, and personal experiences.

3. Reflect Deeply
    - Engage in practices like journaling, meditation, or contemplative prayer to process thoughts and feelings.
4. Stay Open to Change
    - Be willing to let go of beliefs or habits that no longer serve your growth.
5. Connect with Others
    - Share your journey with supportive communities or mentors who encourage exploration.
6. Apply Insights to Life
    - Integrate newfound understanding into daily actions, relationships, and contributions to the world.

Conclusion

The journey from doubt to spiritual insight is a deeply personal yet universally resonant path. By embracing inquiry, individuals can break free from limiting beliefs, expand their understanding, and cultivate a spirituality that is both authentic and inclusive. Questioning becomes not a sign of weakness but a powerful tool for transformation—a means of peeling back layers to reveal deeper truths about oneself and the universe.

As these stories demonstrate, the courage to question and the openness to change can lead to profound personal growth and the ability to impact the world positively. In the tapestry of human experience, each journey adds richness and depth, reminding us that we are all seekers on the path toward greater understanding.

Section 4.3: The Search for Universal Truth

The quest for universal truth is a fundamental aspect of the human experience. It is a journey that often involves navigating the tension between doubt and faith, certainty and uncertainty. In the search for meaning and understanding, individuals are frequently confronted with the limits of reason and the complexities of existence. This section explores how embracing uncertainty can lead to a deeper connection with a larger reality beyond immediate comprehension. Central to this exploration is the philosophy of Søren Kierkegaard, particularly his concept of the existential leap of faith.

Embracing Uncertainty: The Human Condition

Uncertainty is an inherent part of life. Despite advancements in knowledge and technology, there remain questions that elude definitive answers. Matters of existence, purpose, morality, and the divine often reside in realms where empirical evidence is insufficient. The recognition of this uncertainty can be both disconcerting and liberating.

- **Disconcerting**: It challenges the desire for control and predictability.
- **Liberating**: It opens the door to possibilities beyond conventional understanding.

The search for universal truth requires acknowledging the limitations of human reason and embracing the mystery that lies beyond. This acceptance sets the stage for a transformative journey from skepticism to a profound trust in a larger connectedness.

Søren Kierkegaard: The Father of Existentialism

Søren Kierkegaard (1813–1855) was a Danish philosopher, theologian, and writer who is often considered the father of existentialism. His work delved into the complexities of human existence, faith, and the individual's relationship with God. Kierkegaard emphasized the importance of personal choice and commitment in the face of uncertainty.

Key Themes in Kierkegaard's Philosophy

- **Subjectivity and Individuality**: Truth is subjective and must be experienced personally.
- **Existential Anxiety**: The awareness of freedom and responsibility generates anxiety, which is a catalyst for growth.
- **Stages of Life's Way**: The aesthetic, ethical, and religious stages represent different approaches to life.
- **Leap of Faith**: Transcending rational limitations through a passionate commitment to the divine.

The Existential Leap of Faith

The leap of faith is one of Kierkegaard's most influential concepts. It refers to the act of embracing belief in something that cannot be fully justified by reason alone. This leap is not irrational but acknowledges that certain truths lie beyond the scope of logical proof.

Characteristics of the Leap of Faith

- **Embracing Paradox**: Accepting contradictions that cannot be resolved through reason (e.g., the paradox of the incarnation in Christianity).
- **Passionate Commitment**: Involves a deep, personal engagement rather than passive acceptance.
- **Risk and Uncertainty**: Recognizes that faith involves vulnerability and the possibility of doubt.
- **Subjective Truth**: Emphasizes personal experience and inwardness as pathways to truth.

Implications of the Leap

- **Transcending Rational Limits**: Reason has boundaries, and some aspects of existence require a different mode of understanding.
- **Authentic Existence**: By making the leap, individuals move toward a more authentic and meaningful life.
- **Connection with the Divine**: The leap bridges the gap between the finite human and the infinite absolute.

Trusting in a Larger Connectedness

Kierkegaard's leap of faith involves trusting in a reality that transcends immediate understanding. This trust is not blind but is informed by a recognition of one's limitations and a profound yearning for connection with something greater.

Elements of Trusting Beyond Understanding

- **Acceptance of Mystery**: Embracing the unknown as an integral part of existence.
- **Openness to Experience**: Being receptive to insights and revelations that may not fit within conventional frameworks.
- **Integration of Faith and Reason**: Allowing faith to complement reason without disregarding the value of rational thought.
- **Commitment to Personal Growth**: Viewing the leap as a step toward self-realization and fulfillment.

The Journey from Skepticism to Faith

The transition from skepticism to faith is not a rejection of doubt but an integration of doubt into a more expansive understanding. Kierkegaard viewed doubt as essential to faith; without uncertainty, faith loses its meaning.

Stages of the Journey

1. **Recognition of Limitations**: Acknowledging that reason and evidence have boundaries in addressing existential questions.
2. **Encounter with Anxiety**: Facing the discomfort that arises from uncertainty and the freedom to choose.
3. **Decision Point**: Choosing whether to remain in skepticism or to make the leap of faith.
4. **Embracing the Leap**: Committing to belief in the face of uncertainty, leading to a deeper connection with the universal truth.
5. **Ongoing Process**: Understanding that faith is not a one-time event but a continuous journey that involves ongoing reflection and commitment.

Kierkegaard's Three Stages of Life

Kierkegaard outlined three stages or spheres of existence through which individuals may progress:

1. **Aesthetic Stage**: Focused on sensory experiences, pleasure, and the pursuit of personal satisfaction. Characterized by a lack of commitment and constant search for novelty.
2. **Ethical Stage**: Involves a commitment to societal norms, moral duties, and responsibilities. Represents

a higher level of engagement but may still lack personal authenticity.
3. **Religious Stage**: Transcends the ethical by establishing a personal relationship with the divine. Requires the leap of faith and embracing paradoxes.

The movement from the aesthetic through the ethical to the religious stage represents a deepening of the individual's engagement with life and truth.

Paradox and Faith

Kierkegaard emphasized that true faith often involves embracing paradoxes that defy logical explanation. For example, in Christian theology, the concept of Jesus as both fully human and fully divine is a paradox that cannot be fully comprehended through reason alone.

- **Embracing Paradox**: Accepting these contradictions requires moving beyond rationality and trusting in a higher logic.
- **Role of Passion**: Passionate inwardness enables individuals to connect with these paradoxes on a personal level.

Application to Modern Spirituality

Kierkegaard's insights remain relevant to contemporary seekers who grapple with uncertainty and the desire for authentic connection.

Embracing Uncertainty in a Complex World

- **Navigating Complexity**: In an age of information overload and diverse perspectives, embracing uncertainty allows for a more open and flexible approach to spirituality.
- **Integration of Science and Spirituality**: Recognizing the limits of scientific explanation in addressing existential questions can lead to a more holistic understanding.

Personal Commitment and Authenticity

- **Individual Path**: Encourages individuals to forge their own spiritual paths based on personal conviction rather than conforming to external pressures.
- **Authentic Living**: Aligning actions with deeply held beliefs fosters integrity and fulfillment.

Community and Connectedness

- **Shared Journey**: While the leap of faith is personal, it can lead to a sense of connectedness with others who are on similar journeys.
- **Universal Truths**: Trusting in a larger connectedness highlights the commonalities that unite humanity beyond cultural or religious differences.

Challenges and Considerations

Embracing Kierkegaard's leap of faith involves facing certain challenges:

- **Risk of Isolation**: The intensely personal nature of the leap may lead to feelings of isolation from others who do not share the same convictions.
- **Balance Between Faith and Reason**: Finding the equilibrium between embracing mystery and maintaining rational integrity can be difficult.
- **Potential for Despair**: The weight of existential anxiety may lead to despair if not navigated carefully.

Overcoming Challenges

- **Community Support**: Engaging with supportive communities can provide encouragement and shared understanding.
- **Continuous Reflection**: Ongoing self-examination helps maintain balance and prevent stagnation.
- **Embracing Paradox as Growth**: Viewing contradictions as opportunities for growth rather than obstacles.

The Leap as a Universal Metaphor

While rooted in Christian existentialism, the concept of the leap of faith resonates across various spiritual traditions:

- **In Buddhism**: Letting go of attachments and embracing the impermanence of life requires trust in the process of awakening.
- **In Hinduism**: Surrendering to the divine will (bhakti) involves devotion beyond intellectual understanding.
- **In Mysticism**: Direct experiences of the divine often transcend rational explanation, necessitating a leap into the unknown.

Conclusion: Trusting Beyond Understanding

The search for universal truth is a journey that invites individuals to move beyond the confines of certainty and embrace the vastness of the unknown. Kierkegaard's existential leap of faith serves as a powerful metaphor for this journey. It challenges us to:

- **Acknowledge Our Limitations**: Recognize that not all aspects of existence can be grasped by reason alone.
- **Embrace Uncertainty with Courage**: Face the unknown with a spirit of openness and willingness to grow.
- **Trust in a Larger Connectedness**: Believe that there is a unifying reality that binds all things, even if it lies beyond immediate comprehension.
- **Commit to Personal Authenticity**: Live in accordance with deeply held beliefs and values, forging a path that is true to oneself.

By making the leap of faith, we open ourselves to a richer, more meaningful existence. We become participants in the unfolding mystery of life, connected to a universal truth that transcends individual understanding. This journey from skepticism to trust is not a denial of doubt but an integration of doubt into a broader context of faith and connectedness.

Chapter 5: A Unified Vision of Truth

Section 5.1: The One and the Many

One of the most enduring questions in philosophy and spirituality is how to reconcile the diversity of human experience, thought, and belief with the idea of a unified truth. Throughout history, different cultures, religions, and philosophies have provided a variety of answers to the most profound questions of existence: What is the nature of reality? What is our purpose? How do we connect with the divine or the ultimate source of all things? While these answers vary across traditions, many suggest that beneath the surface of this diversity lies a single, ultimate truth.

One of the most compelling frameworks for understanding this idea comes from Plotinus, the founder of Neoplatonism. His philosophical system, developed in the third century CE, presents a vision of reality in which all multiplicity—the many different aspects of life and existence—stems from a single source, which he calls The One. According to Plotinus, all that exists in the universe, from physical objects to the highest forms of thought and spirit, is an emanation from this ultimate source. By exploring this concept, we can see how different philosophies, despite their seeming contradictions, are different paths to the same truth.

The One: Plotinus' Vision of Ultimate Reality

In Plotinus' Neoplatonism, The One is the ultimate reality—beyond being, thought, or language. It is the origin and source of all that exists, but it is not something that can be directly described or comprehended by the human mind. The One is infinite, eternal, and transcendent, but it is also the source of all things, from the highest forms of spiritual consciousness to the physical world we inhabit.

Emanation: The Process of Creation

Plotinus explains the relationship between The One and the diversity of existence through a process he calls emanation. Unlike creation in the Judeo-Christian sense, where God actively creates the world, emanation is a natural, effortless outpouring from The One. Just as light naturally radiates from the sun, so too does everything in existence flow naturally from The One. This process unfolds in a series of stages:

1. **The One**: The ultimate source, beyond all forms and categories. The One is ineffable and cannot be fully grasped by human understanding, but it is the foundation of all that exists.

2. **The Nous (Divine Mind)**: The first emanation from The One. The Nous represents pure intellect, containing within it the perfect forms or ideas, much like Plato's theory of the Forms. The Nous is the realm of pure thought and is the closest to The One in nature.

3. **The Soul**: Emanating from the Nous, the Soul bridges the divine and the material worlds. It animates life, and through it, individuals connect to both higher spiritual realities and the physical world.

4. **The Material World**: The furthest emanation from The One, the material world is characterized by multiplicity and change. However, it is still connected to The One through the Soul and the Nous, though this connection may be less apparent in everyday life.

Each level of emanation reflects The One, but as emanation moves further from the source, it becomes more differentiated and complex. The diversity we observe in the world—different forms of life, thought, and belief—are all manifestations of this original unity. In this way, Plotinus sees the many as fundamentally unified, even if that unity is not immediately apparent.

Truth as a Reflection of The One

From Plotinus' perspective, all truths—whether they come from philosophy, science, religion, or art—are reflections of the same ultimate reality, The One. Just as light can be refracted through a prism to create many different colors, so too can truth be refracted into many different perspectives. While different traditions may emphasize different aspects of reality, they are all, in some way, expressions of the same underlying truth.

Diverse Philosophies, One Truth

Different philosophical traditions offer different paths to understanding the ultimate nature of reality. For Plotinus, these different paths are not contradictory but complementary. Each tradition, whether it focuses on reason, ethics, spirituality, or science, provides a glimpse of the ultimate truth. Some may focus on the material world, while others may focus on the mind or the spirit, but all are reflections of the same source.

- **Western Philosophy**: Traditions like **Platonism**, **Aristotelianism**, and later **existentialism** explore different facets of human existence, from the nature of reality and forms to the meaning of human freedom and purpose. Each of these philosophies contributes a piece to the larger puzzle of truth.
- **Eastern Philosophy**: In **Hinduism** and **Buddhism**, the focus is often on the realization of unity with the divine or the dissolution of the ego in the experience of enlightenment. These traditions, like Neoplatonism, emphasize the importance of transcending the material world to achieve a higher understanding of reality.
- **Science and Rational Inquiry**: In the modern world, science plays a crucial role in uncovering truths about the physical universe. While science often focuses on the material world, it too is a path toward understanding the underlying principles that govern reality.

Unity in Diversity

Plotinus' concept of emanation helps us understand how different traditions can appear to offer different truths, yet still be part of a unified whole. Just as different parts of the body serve different functions but are all part of the same organism, so too do different philosophies serve different roles in understanding the same ultimate reality. Diversity is not a sign of disconnection but a reflection of the richness and complexity of The One.

Spiritual and Philosophical Paths to Unity

Many spiritual traditions also reflect this idea of unity in diversity. They teach that while human beings may experience the world in different ways, we are all connected to the same ultimate reality, and our various spiritual practices are simply different ways of returning to that source.

Hinduism: Unity Through Realization of Brahman

In Hinduism, the concept of Brahman closely parallels Plotinus' notion of The One. Brahman is the ultimate, formless reality that underlies all existence. While Brahman can manifest in many forms, such as the gods and goddesses of the Hindu pantheon, it remains one, indivisible truth. The spiritual goal in Hinduism is to recognize that the individual soul (**Atman**) is not separate from Brahman but is, in fact, identical with it.

- **Jnana Yoga** (The Path of Knowledge) focuses on intellectual and philosophical inquiry to realize the unity of Atman and Brahman. Through study, meditation, and contemplation, practitioners seek to transcend the illusion of multiplicity and experience the oneness of reality.

Buddhism: The Interconnectedness of All Things

In Buddhism, the idea of interconnectedness reflects a similar understanding of unity. Dependent origination, the principle that all things arise in relation to other things, shows that nothing exists in isolation. While Buddhism does not focus on a single, transcendent source like The One or Brahman, it teaches that all phenomena are interconnected and that the experience of this interconnectedness is key to liberation from suffering.

- **Meditation** in Buddhism is a tool for realizing the interconnected nature of reality and dissolving the illusion of separateness. By observing the impermanence and interdependence of all things, practitioners come to understand the unity that underlies the apparent multiplicity of life.

Christianity: Unity in the Body of Christ

Christianity also emphasizes unity, particularly through the concept of the Body of Christ. In the New Testament, Paul writes that all Christians are united in Christ, even though they may come from different backgrounds and serve different roles within the Church. This idea of spiritual unity echoes Plotinus' notion of the many emanating from The One, with Christ as the unifying force that connects all believers.

- **Christian Mysticism**: Mystical traditions within Christianity, such as the writings of Meister Eckhart and Julian of Norwich, emphasize the idea of unity with God. For these mystics, the experience of divine love and union with God reflects the same Neoplatonic vision of returning to the source.

Returning to The One: The Path of Spiritual Ascent

Plotinus' Neoplatonism does not just describe the emanation of the many from The One—it also provides a roadmap for the return to The One. This process of spiritual ascent involves turning away from the distractions of the material world and focusing on the inner journey toward unity with the divine source. Plotinus describes this process as a gradual ascent through the stages of existence, from the material world to the Soul, the Nous, and finally to The One.

The Practice of Contemplation

The key to this ascent, according to Plotinus, is contemplation. By engaging in deep, focused contemplation, individuals can move beyond the sensory world and begin to connect with the higher realms of the Soul and the Nous. Contemplation allows the soul to turn inward, away from the multiplicity of the external world, and toward the unity of The One.

- **Spiritual Practices Across Traditions**: This process of ascent through contemplation is echoed in many spiritual traditions, from **meditation** in Buddhism and **yoga** in Hinduism to **prayer** and **mystical contemplation** in Christianity and Islam. In each case, the goal is to transcend the ordinary world of multiplicity and experience the unity of the divine.

Conclusion: The One and the Many as a Unified Vision of Truth

Plotinus' vision of The One and the many offers a profound way of understanding the relationship between diversity and unity. By seeing all things as emanations from a single source, we can appreciate the richness of human thought, belief, and experience without losing sight of the deeper unity that underlies them. Whether we approach truth through philosophy, science, religion, or art, we are all ultimately seeking to reconnect with The One—the ultimate source of all that exists.

In a world that often seems fragmented and divided, Plotinus' Neoplatonism reminds us that this diversity is not a sign of disunity but a reflection of the many ways in which the ultimate truth can be experienced and understood. Each path, whether it emphasizes reason, faith, or contemplation, is a step toward the same goal: the realization of our connection to the divine source and the unity of all things.

Section 5.2: The Role of Unity in Religion

Throughout history, religions have offered diverse approaches to understanding the nature of existence, the divine, and the human spirit. While each tradition has its own unique teachings and practices, they all point toward a shared purpose: connecting the individual with a larger, transcendent reality. Huston Smith, a renowned scholar of comparative religion, dedicated his work to revealing how the world's major religions, despite their differences, ultimately guide humanity toward a unified truth.

In his landmark book, *The World's Religions*, Smith explored the rich diversity of spiritual traditions—Hinduism, Buddhism, Judaism, Christianity, Islam, Taoism, and Confucianism—and highlighted the common thread that runs through them. According to Smith, while each religion offers its own path, their ultimate goal is the same: to transcend the ego and connect with a higher reality. This section will examine how practices such as meditation, prayer, and rituals serve as methods of connecting individuals to the unified truth that lies at the heart of all spiritual traditions.

Huston Smith's Vision: Unity in Diversity

Huston Smith viewed the world's religions as complementary, each offering different perspectives on the same ultimate reality. Rather than seeing these religions as conflicting, Smith believed they were multiple pathways leading to the same goal—union with the transcendent. He emphasized that despite the outer differences in beliefs and rituals, at their core, religions share a common purpose: to align the individual with the divine or universal truth.

Religions as Pathways to the Same Truth

Smith argued that all religions, in their own way, seek to answer the same fundamental questions: What is the nature of existence? What is our purpose? How can we connect with the divine? Each tradition offers a unique lens through which to explore these questions, but the destination remains the same—transcendence of the self and connection with a higher reality.

- Unity in Purpose: Smith highlighted that the ultimate purpose of all spiritual traditions is to transform the individual. Whether through prayer, meditation, or acts of devotion, each religion offers tools for transcending the ego and experiencing oneness with the divine source that underlies all existence.

- **Transcendence of the Ego:** The various practices across religions are designed to dissolve the illusion of separateness and help individuals realize their interconnectedness with all beings and the divine. This spiritual transformation leads to a greater awareness of the unity that pervades all of existence.

By emphasizing the shared goal of spiritual transformation, Smith revealed how the world's religions, despite their external differences, point toward a common truth: the unity of all things within the divine.

Practices as Pathways to Unity

Religious practices such as meditation, prayer, and rituals are central to connecting individuals with the divine or universal truth. These practices, though unique to each tradition, serve as methods for transcending ordinary experience and realizing the unity that binds all of existence. Let's explore how some of the world's major religions use these practices to connect with the divine.

Meditation: Quieting the Mind to Connect with the Divine

Meditation is a foundational practice in many religious traditions, particularly in Hinduism, Buddhism, and Taoism. Through meditation, practitioners quiet the mind, turn inward, and transcend the distractions of everyday life, ultimately connecting with a deeper spiritual reality. Huston Smith viewed meditation as a powerful tool for spiritual awakening, one that leads individuals toward an experience of the oneness that pervades all things.

- Hinduism: In Hinduism, meditation is used to realize the unity of the individual soul (Atman) with the ultimate reality (Brahman). Practices like Raja Yoga guide practitioners through stages of meditation that dissolve the ego and help them experience the oneness of all existence.
- Buddhism: In Buddhist meditation, practices such as Vipassana and Zen help practitioners cultivate mindfulness and insight into the nature of reality. By observing the interdependence of all phenomena, Buddhists come to recognize that the self is an illusion, and that all beings are interconnected in a larger, unified whole.

- Taoism: In Taoism, meditation helps individuals align themselves with the Tao, the natural flow of the universe. By practicing stillness and non-action (wu wei), Taoists seek harmony with the Tao, recognizing that they are part of an interconnected and unified cosmic order.

Prayer: Communing with the Divine

Prayer is a universal practice across religious traditions, serving as a way for individuals to communicate with the divine. Through prayer, believers express their devotion, seek guidance, and open themselves to the presence of a higher power. Huston Smith saw prayer as a direct means of connecting with the transcendent, a practice that helps bridge the gap between the individual and the divine source.

- Christianity: In Christianity, prayer is central to spiritual life. Whether through formal prayers like the Lord's Prayer or contemplative practices, Christians seek communion with God, striving to align their hearts and minds with the divine will. Prayer allows believers to experience God's presence and connect with the divine love that unites all things.

- Islam: In Islam, the practice of Salat, or the five daily prayers, is a sacred ritual that connects Muslims with God throughout the day. By turning toward Mecca and reciting specific prayers, Muslims reaffirm their submission to the will of God and their unity with the larger Islamic community. Prayer in Islam is a profound expression of the oneness of God (Tawhid).

- Judaism: In Judaism, prayer is both a communal and individual practice that reinforces the believer's relationship with God. The recitation of prayers such as the Shema—"Hear, O Israel: The Lord our God, the Lord is One"—emphasizes the unity of God and invites worshippers to live in alignment with this divine oneness.

Rituals: Embodying Unity Through Sacred Acts

Rituals are an essential aspect of religious practice, serving as physical expressions of spiritual truths. They help individuals embody their beliefs and connect with the divine through sacred actions. For Huston Smith, rituals are powerful tools for creating a sense of unity, both within the individual and within the community.

- Hinduism: In Hindu rituals such as puja, offerings are made to deities as a way of honoring the divine presence in all things. These rituals serve to remind practitioners of their connection to the cosmos and the divine essence that permeates the universe.
- Christianity: The Eucharist, or communion, is a central Christian ritual that symbolizes unity with Christ. By partaking in the bread and wine, which represent the body and blood of Christ, Christians participate in an act of spiritual unity with God and with one another.
- Judaism: The observance of Shabbat is a weekly ritual in Judaism that sanctifies time and space. Through the lighting of candles and recitation of prayers, Jews reconnect with the divine and recognize the unity of creation. Shabbat is a reminder of the sacred covenant between God and humanity.
- Buddhism: In Buddhist rituals like Vesak, which celebrates the birth, enlightenment, and death of the Buddha, practitioners come together in collective

acts of devotion. These rituals reflect the interconnectedness of all beings and the shared journey toward enlightenment.

Transformation and Unity: The Goal of Spiritual Practice

For Huston Smith, the ultimate purpose of religious practices is spiritual transformation—the process of transcending the limitations of the ego and experiencing unity with the divine. Whether through meditation, prayer, or ritual, the goal is to help individuals recognize that they are not separate from one another or from the divine source of all existence. By engaging in these practices, people are invited to move beyond the illusion of separateness and embrace the reality of oneness.

Dissolution of the Ego

In many religious traditions, spiritual practices are designed to dissolve the ego, the false sense of self that creates the illusion of separation. Through prayer, meditation, and ritual, practitioners come to realize that their individual identity is part of a greater whole.

- Buddhism: The practice of meditation leads to the dissolution of the ego and the realization of Anatta (no-self), helping practitioners understand that they are interconnected with all beings.
- Sufism: In Sufism, the mystical branch of Islam, the practice of dhikr (remembrance of God) leads to fana—the annihilation of the self in the love of God. This spiritual practice allows Sufis to experience union with the divine and recognize their oneness with all creation.
- Hinduism: Through the various paths of yoga, practitioners seek to transcend the limitations of the ego and experience union with Brahman, the ultimate reality that connects all things.

Unity of All Religions

Huston Smith argued that the world's religions, despite their external differences, ultimately share the same goal: to help individuals transcend the ego and experience the unity that connects all beings. By focusing on the common purpose of spiritual transformation, Smith showed how all religions are part of a larger spiritual tradition that seeks to guide humanity toward the same truth—**the oneness of existence.**

Section 5.3: Love as a Universal Principle

Throughout history, mystics and spiritual teachers have pointed to love as a universal force that transcends individual experiences, uniting all beings with one another and with the divine source of existence. No one has captured this vision of love more beautifully than the 13th-century Persian poet and Sufi mystic Rumi. In his poetry, Rumi speaks of love not simply as an emotion, but as a metaphysical principle—a force that underlies all reality and binds everything in the universe together. For Rumi, love is the essential thread that connects the human soul to the divine and serves as the pathway to realizing the unity of all creation.

In this section, we explore Rumi's portrayal of love as a profound, cosmic force. For Rumi, love is the driving energy behind all existence, and through love, one can transcend the boundaries of the self and experience a direct connection to the source of all life.

Rumi's Vision of Love as a Metaphysical Truth

Rumi's poetry transcends the personal, romantic notions of love often associated with the word, offering instead a vision of love as a universal and divine force. In the Sufi tradition, love is seen as the means by which the soul reunites with its divine origin. Love, in Rumi's eyes, is the force that moves the universe, leading all beings back to their source—the Beloved, which is often a metaphor for God or the ultimate reality.

Love as the Force That Animates the Universe

Rumi believed that love is the fundamental energy that powers the universe. In his view, everything in creation is motivated by love—whether the turning of the planets, the growth of a flower, or the yearning of the human soul for God. One of Rumi's famous lines captures this beautifully:

"Love is the bridge between you and everything."

In this simple yet profound statement, Rumi suggests that love is the connecting force between all things, dissolving the illusion of separation. It is the force that binds us to one another and to the divine. Without love, there is no life, no motion, no meaning.

- Love as Creation: In Sufi cosmology, the universe itself was created out of God's love. Love is not an abstract concept but the very foundation of existence. Rumi's poetry frequently references this idea, portraying the world as an expression of divine love that is always calling souls back to their source.

Love as the Path to Unity with the Divine

In Rumi's spiritual philosophy, love is the key to experiencing oneness with God. The human soul, according to Rumi, is separated from its divine origin and experiences a deep longing to return. This separation creates a yearning that can only be fulfilled through the transformative power of love.

- The Beloved as the Divine: Throughout Rumi's work, the Beloved is often a symbol for God or the ultimate source of reality. The soul's desire for the Beloved represents its longing to return to the divine. In one of his most famous lines, Rumi writes: *"The minute I heard my first love story, I started looking for you, not knowing how blind that was. Lovers don't finally meet somewhere. They're in each other all along."*

This line speaks to the idea that the soul's search for love is, in fact, a search for unity with the divine. The journey to find love outside of oneself ultimately leads back to the realization that love—and the divine—have always been within.

- Union with the Divine: For Rumi, love is the means by which the soul dissolves the boundaries of the self and merges with the divine. This is not simply an emotional experience, but a mystical union in which the soul becomes one with the source of all existence. This process is known in Sufism as fana, or annihilation of the self in God's love.

Love as a Universal Force Binding All Things

Beyond the personal experience of love, Rumi's poetry emphasizes the universal nature of this force. Love, in his view, transcends individual relationships and connects all beings—human, animal, and cosmic—to one another. It is through love that the interconnectedness of all life becomes apparent.

Love Dissolves the Illusion of Separation

One of the key messages in Rumi's poetry is that love has the power to dissolve the illusion of separation between the self and others, and between humanity and the divine. In one of his poems, Rumi writes:

"All loves are a bridge to divine love. Yet, those who have not had a taste of it want to remain in the shelter of duality."

In this passage, Rumi points out that all forms of love—whether romantic, familial, or spiritual—are reflections of the same divine love. When we truly experience love, we recognize that there is no separation between us and others. The boundaries between the lover and the beloved fade away, revealing the underlying unity of all existence.

- Transcending Duality: Rumi's work frequently addresses the concept of duality, which he sees as an illusion. The material world, with its distinctions and divisions, creates the false impression that we are separate from one another and from God. Love, according to Rumi, transcends this duality, revealing the oneness of all things.
- Love as the Unifying Principle: Through love, we come to see that we are not isolated beings but part

of a greater whole. In one of his most famous lines, Rumi writes:

"You are not a drop in the ocean. You are the entire ocean, in a drop."

This metaphor beautifully captures the essence of Rumi's vision: each of us is part of the greater reality, and through love, we come to realize our unity with the divine and with all of creation.

Love as a Metaphysical Truth Across Traditions

Rumi's vision of love as a universal force that binds all of existence is not unique to Sufism. Many of the world's great religious and philosophical traditions recognize love as a central metaphysical truth—a force that transcends individual emotions and connects all beings to one another and to the divine.

Christianity: Love as the Essence of God

In Christianity, love is often viewed as the highest expression of divine truth. Agape—unconditional love—is considered the purest form of love and is central to Jesus' teachings. Jesus' command to "love your neighbor as yourself" reflects the idea that love is the bond that connects all people, and by loving others, we come closer to God.

- Union with God Through Love: Christian mystics like St. John of the Cross and Julian of Norwich describe the experience of union with God as a process of surrendering to divine love. For them, love is not just an emotion but the very force that unites the soul with God in mystical communion.

Hinduism: Bhakti as Love for the Divine

In Hinduism, the path of Bhakti Yoga emphasizes love and devotion to the divine as a means of spiritual liberation. Through acts of devotion, prayer, and surrender, practitioners seek to experience the divine presence in their hearts and to dissolve the barriers between themselves and God.

- Love as Liberation: In Bhakti Yoga, love for God is seen as the ultimate path to moksha, or liberation. This love transcends personal desires and ego, leading to a direct experience of oneness with the divine.

Buddhism: Compassion as Universal Love

In Buddhism, the concept of Metta (loving-kindness) and Karuna (compassion) are central teachings. While Buddhism does not personify love as a deity, it emphasizes the cultivation of compassion as a means of realizing the interconnectedness of all beings. By extending love and kindness to others, Buddhists aim to transcend the ego and recognize the unity that underlies all life.

- Compassion as a Path to Enlightenment: For Buddhists, the practice of loving-kindness meditation helps dissolve the illusion of separation, promoting a sense of unity with all living beings. Through compassion, one experiences the interconnectedness of life and moves closer to spiritual awakening.

Conclusion: Love as the Unifying Force of Existence

Rumi's poetry invites us to see love not merely as an emotion but as a universal principle—a metaphysical force that permeates the entire cosmos. Love, in Rumi's vision, is the energy that moves all things, the bridge between the human and the divine, the force that dissolves the illusion of separateness and reveals the unity of all existence. By embracing love in its fullest sense, we come to understand that we are all connected—both to one another and to the source of all life.

In the teachings of Rumi and other spiritual traditions, love is the path to transformation, leading us beyond the ego and into the realization of oneness. Whether through acts of devotion, compassion, or mystical surrender, love is the doorway to the divine, guiding us toward a deeper experience of the truth that unites all of existence.

Chapter 6: The Universal Language of Spirituality

Section 6.1: Spiritual Practices Across Cultures

Throughout history, cultures and religious traditions have developed diverse spiritual practices to connect with the universal source—whether it is called God, Brahman, Tao, or simply the essence of existence. Despite their surface differences, these practices share a common goal: transcending the limitations of the ego, deepening the connection to the divine, and fostering unity with the world. Whether through meditation, prayer, fasting, or rituals, spiritual practices across various traditions express a universal longing for communion with something greater than the self.

A key figure who bridges spiritual traditions and emphasizes the universal nature of such practices is the Vietnamese Buddhist monk and peace activist Thich Nhat Hanh. His teachings on mindfulness show that the essence of spirituality is not bound by one specific tradition but can be experienced by anyone, anywhere, through conscious attention to the present moment. In this section, we will explore how spiritual practices from different cultures and religions, despite their unique forms, serve the same fundamental purpose: connecting the individual with the universal source of life.

Meditation: Silence and Stillness Across Traditions

Meditation is perhaps the most universal spiritual practice, found in almost every religious tradition. At its core, meditation involves turning inward, calming the mind, and transcending the distractions of daily life to connect with a deeper reality. While the specific methods and purposes of meditation vary across cultures, the practice consistently aims to still the mind and foster a sense of unity with the divine or the present moment.

Buddhism: Meditation as Mindfulness and Insight

In Buddhism, meditation is central to the spiritual path, with practices such as Vipassana (insight meditation) and Zen helping practitioners cultivate mindfulness and awareness of the present moment. Thich Nhat Hanh emphasizes the power of mindfulness as a way to fully inhabit each moment, seeing it as a portal to deeper spiritual awareness. For him, mindfulness is not confined to seated meditation but is a way of life, allowing practitioners to connect with the universal source by being fully present with themselves and the world around them.

- Mindfulness of Breath: In his teachings, Thich Nhat Hanh stresses the simplicity and accessibility of meditation, often focusing on the breath. "Breathing in, I calm my body. Breathing out, I smile." These simple words reveal how mindfulness, when practiced with intention, becomes a means of reconnecting with life itself—an experience shared by all beings, regardless of tradition.

Hinduism: Meditation as Union with Brahman

In Hinduism, meditation is a means of realizing the unity of the individual soul (Atman) with the universal reality (Brahman). Through practices such as Jnana Yoga (the path of knowledge) or Raja Yoga (the royal path of meditation), Hindus seek to quiet the mind and dissolve the illusion of separateness, ultimately experiencing the oneness of all things.

- Chanting and Mantra Meditation: Mantra meditation, in which practitioners repeat sacred sounds like Om or the Gayatri Mantra, serves as a way to align the practitioner's mind with the vibrations of the universe. Through this practice, the individual moves beyond intellectual understanding to direct experience of the divine presence in all things.

Christianity: Contemplative Prayer and Union with God

In Christian mysticism, meditation often takes the form of contemplative prayer, a practice of silently resting in the presence of God. Saints like St. Teresa of Avila and St. John of the Cross describe contemplative prayer as a way of quieting the mind and heart to allow the soul to commune with God.

- Centering Prayer: A modern Christian practice, centering prayer, emphasizes stillness and the use of a sacred word or phrase to focus the mind. Through this silent repetition, the practitioner lets go of thoughts and distractions, creating a space for divine union.

Taoism: Meditation and Harmony with the Tao

In Taoism, meditation is a way to align with the Tao—the natural flow of the universe. Taoist meditation practices, like Zuo Wang (sitting and forgetting), encourage practitioners to empty the mind of desires and worries, allowing them to return to their natural state of balance and harmony with the Tao.

- Wu Wei: The concept of wu wei, or effortless action, is a form of meditative practice in itself. By aligning with the Tao, one acts without forcing or striving, allowing life to flow naturally. In this state, the practitioner connects with the universal source through a deep sense of harmony with the natural world.

Prayer: Reaching Out to the Divine

Prayer, like meditation, is a universal spiritual practice that transcends religious boundaries. Whether through spoken words, silent contemplation, or heartfelt devotion, prayer is a way for individuals to communicate with the divine and express their deepest desires, hopes, and gratitude. Across cultures, prayer serves as a method of aligning the individual's will with the greater forces of the universe.

Islam: Salat and Submission to God

In Islam, Salat, the five daily prayers, is central to spiritual life. These prayers, performed at specific times throughout the day, serve as a reminder of the believer's connection to God. Through prayer, Muslims express their submission to Allah and acknowledge their place within the divine order of creation.

- The Act of Prostration: In Salat, the act of prostration—bowing down to the ground in submission—symbolizes the believer's surrender to the will of God. This physical gesture reflects the spiritual reality of humility and the recognition that all life is sustained by the divine.

Christianity: Petition, Thanksgiving, and Praise

In Christianity, prayer takes many forms, from personal petitions and expressions of gratitude to communal acts of worship and praise. The Lord's Prayer, taught by Jesus, is one of the most well-known prayers in the Christian tradition, offering a model for how believers can align themselves with God's will.

- Prayer as Communion: For Christians, prayer is not only a request for divine intervention but also an opportunity for intimate communion with God. Whether in moments of private reflection or in the context of communal worship, prayer is a way of deepening one's connection with the divine source of life.

Judaism: Daily Prayer and the Shema

In Judaism, daily prayer is a way of keeping God at the center of life. The recitation of the Shema—"Hear, O Israel: The Lord our God, the Lord is One"—is a declaration of faith in the unity of God and a reminder of the Jewish people's covenant with the divine.

- Kavanah and Intention: Jewish prayer emphasizes the importance of kavanah, or intention. It is not the words of the prayer alone that matter, but the inner focus and devotion with which the prayer is offered. In this way, prayer becomes a channel for connecting with God's presence in every moment.

Fasting: Physical Discipline as a Path to Spiritual Awareness

Fasting is another universal practice that appears in various religious traditions as a way of purifying the body and mind, creating space for spiritual insight, and deepening one's connection to the divine. Through fasting, individuals temporarily set aside physical needs to focus on spiritual realities.

Islam: Ramadan and the Practice of Self-Discipline

During the holy month of Ramadan, Muslims fast from dawn until sunset, refraining from food, drink, and other physical pleasures. This period of fasting is not only a test of self-discipline but also a time of spiritual reflection and increased devotion to God. Fasting during Ramadan helps Muslims cultivate a sense of gratitude for life's blessings and a deeper awareness of their dependence on God.

- Breaking the Fast (Iftar): The communal breaking of the fast at sunset, known as Iftar, serves as a reminder of the interconnectedness of the community and the shared experience of devotion. Through fasting, Muslims connect with God and with one another, recognizing that their physical hunger reflects a deeper spiritual longing.

Christianity: Fasting During Lent

In Christianity, fasting is most commonly observed during Lent, a period of 40 days leading up to Easter. During this time, Christians often abstain from certain foods or pleasures as a way of preparing their hearts for the celebration of Christ's resurrection.

- Fasting as Repentance: Fasting during Lent is seen as a way of participating in Christ's suffering and reflecting on one's own spiritual journey. By setting aside physical comforts, Christians create space for repentance and deeper communion with God.

Buddhism: Fasting as a Way to Clarity

In Buddhism, fasting is sometimes used as a tool for developing clarity of mind and detachment from the desires of the body. Monks and laypeople alike may engage in periods of fasting as part of their spiritual practice, recognizing that the body's cravings can be a source of distraction from the pursuit of enlightenment.

- Moderation and the Middle Way: While fasting is practiced, Buddhism emphasizes the Middle Way, avoiding extremes of indulgence or deprivation. Fasting, when undertaken mindfully, helps practitioners cultivate self-awareness and balance.

Rituals: Embodying Sacred Truths

Rituals play an essential role in religious life, offering a way to embody spiritual principles and connect with the divine through sacred actions. Rituals often mark important moments in life—birth, marriage, death—or significant points in the spiritual calendar. Across traditions, rituals serve as a reminder of the larger truths that govern the universe and provide a way for individuals to participate in the sacred order.

Hinduism: Puja and Devotion

In Hinduism, puja is the ritual worship of deities, involving offerings of flowers, food, and incense. Through these acts of devotion, practitioners honor the presence of the divine in their lives and reaffirm their connection to Brahman, the ultimate reality.

- Darshan: One of the key aspects of puja is darshan, the act of seeing and being seen by the deity. This exchange of sight is believed to bless the devotee and foster a sense of closeness to the divine presence.

Catholicism: The Eucharist as Communion

In Catholicism, the Eucharist is the central ritual of the Mass, in which the bread and wine are consecrated and believed to become the body and blood of Christ. This ritual symbolizes the believer's union with Christ and the wider Christian community, reflecting the idea that all are part of the same divine body.

- Transcendence Through Sacrament: The Eucharist serves as a moment of transcendence, where the divine and the earthly meet. Through participation in this sacred ritual, Catholics connect with the mystery of Christ's sacrifice and experience the ongoing presence of God in their lives.

Buddhism: The Offering of Incense

In Buddhist temples, the offering of incense is a common ritual, symbolizing the purification of the mind and the cultivation of virtue. As the smoke rises, it carries the practitioner's intentions toward enlightenment, reminding them of their interconnectedness with the world and the impermanence of all things.

Conclusion: A Universal Language of Spirituality

Spiritual practices across cultures and religions, despite their outward differences, all point to the same ultimate goal: connecting with the universal source. Whether through meditation, prayer, fasting, or rituals, these practices offer ways for individuals to transcend the ego, experience unity with the divine, and cultivate a sense of interconnectedness with all life. As Thich Nhat Hanh reminds us, spirituality is not bound by tradition or doctrine—it is the lived experience of mindfulness, compassion, and presence in each moment. Through these practices, we come to understand that, at the deepest level, we are all part of the same universal truth.

Section 6.2: The Sacred and the Secular

In today's increasingly interconnected world, the boundaries between the sacred and the secular are becoming more fluid. While traditional religions and spiritual practices have long served as pathways to connect with the divine, modern spirituality often transcends these boundaries, offering new ways to experience the sacred in everyday life. This blurring of lines reflects a growing trend in which spirituality is no longer confined to specific rituals or religious contexts but is seen as a universal, accessible experience available to all, regardless of faith or background.

One of the thinkers who has deeply influenced modern views on this subject is the philosopher and mystic Alan Watts. Through his discussions on mysticism, Watts reframed spirituality as something that extends beyond the dogmas of organized religion, emphasizing that the sacred can be found within the ordinary and that mysticism is not limited to religious traditions. For Watts, spirituality is universal and can be embraced by anyone, regardless of whether they adhere to a particular religious path.

In this section, we will explore how the line between the sacred and the secular has become blurred in modern life, how spirituality can be understood outside of traditional religious frameworks, and how figures like Alan Watts have helped to broaden the understanding of mysticism in a way that makes it relevant to contemporary seekers.

The Blurring of Sacred and Secular in Modern Life

Historically, the sacred and the secular have often been viewed as distinct realms. The sacred was reserved for religious settings—places of worship, rituals, and prayers—while the secular referred to the world outside of religion, encompassing work, politics, and the mundane aspects of daily life. However, in the modern world, these distinctions have begun to dissolve. Spirituality is increasingly being woven into the fabric of everyday life, with many people finding ways to integrate the sacred into their secular experiences.

The Sacred in Everyday Moments

As modern spirituality evolves, people are recognizing that the sacred is not confined to specific places or practices but can be encountered in the ordinary moments of life. This shift reflects a broader understanding of sacredness—one that is not dependent on religious institutions but is found in the present moment, in nature, in creativity, and in relationships.

- Mindfulness as Sacred Presence: Practices like mindfulness and meditation, popularized in secular contexts, encourage individuals to bring a sense of sacred attention to the present moment. Whether at work, in conversation, or simply walking in nature, mindfulness allows people to experience the sacredness of life as it unfolds. This mirrors the teachings of Thich Nhat Hanh, who describes mindfulness as a way of being fully present and aware, turning everyday moments into opportunities for spiritual awakening.

- Art and Creativity as Sacred Expression: Many people today find spirituality through art, music, and other creative endeavors. The act of creating, whether through painting, writing, or playing music, becomes a way of tapping into something greater than oneself, a channel for expressing the divine through secular means. For modern seekers, creativity serves as a bridge between the sacred and the secular, allowing them to experience moments of transcendence without the need for traditional religious practices.

Spirituality in Secular Spaces

In the contemporary world, spirituality is increasingly making its way into secular spaces—corporate environments, schools, wellness centers, and public discourse. Concepts like mindfulness, gratitude, and self-compassion, once confined to religious teachings, are now being embraced by people from all walks of life as tools for personal growth and well-being.

- Mindfulness in Corporate and Educational Settings: The rise of mindfulness in the workplace and in schools reflects this blending of sacred and secular values. What was once considered a religious or spiritual practice has now been widely adopted in secular environments as a way to reduce stress, improve focus, and cultivate emotional intelligence. The practice may no longer carry religious overtones, but it retains its spiritual essence—a tool for connecting more deeply with oneself and the present moment.
- Wellness and Spirituality: The global wellness movement also illustrates how secular spaces have become infused with spiritual practices. Yoga studios, meditation retreats, and wellness workshops often draw on ancient spiritual traditions while

presenting them in ways that are accessible to people of all backgrounds. These spaces encourage personal reflection, healing, and connection to something greater, even if the language used is not explicitly religious.

Alan Watts: Mysticism Beyond Religion

One of the key figures who helped to redefine spirituality and blur the line between the sacred and the secular is the philosopher Alan Watts. Watts, known for his ability to bridge Eastern and Western philosophies, challenged the idea that mysticism and spiritual experiences must be tied to organized religion. Instead, he presented spirituality as a universal experience available to anyone, regardless of their religious beliefs or lack thereof.

Mysticism as a Universal Experience

For Watts, mysticism was not a religious doctrine or a set of beliefs, but a way of directly experiencing the divine or ultimate reality. He emphasized that this experience is not limited to saints, monks, or religious practitioners but is accessible to everyone. Watts described mysticism as a way of seeing through the illusion of separateness, allowing individuals to realize their connection to the larger cosmos.

- Transcending Religious Boundaries: Watts argued that while religious traditions offer valuable insights and practices, they are not the only means to experience mysticism. One does not need to belong to a specific faith to have a mystical experience. In fact, Watts often critiqued the rigid structures of organized religion, suggesting that they could sometimes obscure the mystical experience by focusing too much on rules and dogma. Instead, he encouraged people to look beyond religious boundaries and embrace the mystery of existence directly.
- The Here and Now: A central theme in Watts' teachings is the importance of being fully present in the here and now. He believed that mystical experiences are not reserved for the distant future or for an afterlife but can be found in the present moment. By cultivating awareness and openness to life as it unfolds, individuals can touch the sacred in the midst of their everyday, secular lives.

The Sacred in the Ordinary

Watts also emphasized that the sacred can be found in the ordinary moments of life. Rather than viewing spirituality as something that only happens in a church, temple, or sacred space, he suggested that the divine is present in everything—in nature, in relationships, and in the simple act of being alive.

- Nature as a Gateway to the Divine: Watts often spoke of the natural world as a reflection of the sacred. He believed that by contemplating the beauty and interconnectedness of nature, people could experience a sense of awe and wonder that connects them to the greater whole. This idea resonates with modern spirituality, where many individuals find sacredness in nature walks, hiking, or simply sitting by the ocean.
- The Play of Life: Watts described life as a kind of cosmic dance, where every moment is an opportunity to participate in the unfolding of the universe. For him, the spiritual path was not about renouncing the world or escaping from secular life but about embracing the fullness of life, with all its joys and challenges, as an expression of the divine.

Modern Mysticism: Accessible to Everyone

One of the most important contributions of modern mystics like Alan Watts is their emphasis on the accessibility of spirituality. By blurring the line between the sacred and the secular, they have made mysticism more inclusive, allowing people from all walks of life to experience a deeper connection to themselves, the world, and the divine.

Spirituality Without Dogma

For many modern seekers, spirituality is no longer about adhering to a specific set of religious beliefs or practices. Instead, it is about cultivating a personal relationship with the sacred, however that may be defined. This shift reflects a broader movement toward spiritual independence, where individuals draw from multiple traditions and philosophies to create their own spiritual paths.

- Eclectic Spirituality: In the modern world, it is common for individuals to blend elements of Buddhism, Christian mysticism, yoga, and secular mindfulness into a single spiritual practice. This eclectic approach allows people to find meaning in the practices that resonate with them, without being confined to one tradition.

- Mysticism for All: As Watts suggested, mysticism is not an exclusive domain reserved for religious practitioners—it is an open invitation for anyone who seeks a deeper understanding of life. The rise of practices like mindfulness, meditation, and even the growing interest in psychedelics for spiritual exploration, all reflect a shift toward democratizing the mystical experience.

Conclusion: The Universal Sacred

The boundary between the sacred and the secular has become increasingly blurred as modern spirituality continues to evolve. Practices that were once confined to religious traditions—such as meditation, prayer, and mindfulness—are now widely embraced in secular contexts, offering people new ways to experience the sacred in everyday life. Thinkers like Alan Watts have played a crucial role in this transformation, reframing mysticism as a universal experience that transcends religious boundaries and is accessible to everyone.

In this new paradigm, the sacred is no longer confined to specific places or rituals but is present in every moment, available to anyone who is open to it. As Watts and other modern mystics remind us, the path to the divine is not somewhere far away—it is right here, in the midst of the ordinary. By embracing this expanded understanding of spirituality, we come to see that the sacred is not separate from the secular, but woven into the very fabric of life itself.

Section 6.3: The Role of Rituals in Uniting Us

Rituals have been an essential part of human culture for millennia, serving as communal expressions that connect individuals to something greater than themselves. Whether sacred or secular, rituals offer a way to mark significant moments in life, reinforce bonds within a community, and express our collective need for meaning and connection. From weddings and funerals to holidays and cultural celebrations, rituals allow us to participate in a shared experience that transcends individual differences, reminding us of our common humanity and our connection to the larger forces that shape life.

Though rituals vary greatly across cultures and religions, they fulfill a universal function: they provide structure to life's transitions, offer comfort in times of uncertainty, and create space for reflection on the mysteries of existence. Regardless of belief systems, rituals bring people together, fostering a sense of belonging and unity. This section will explore the unifying power of rituals, examining how they serve as a bridge between the individual and the collective, and how they offer a space for us to connect with something beyond ourselves.

The Universal Role of Rituals

Rituals are not just confined to religious settings; they are present in both sacred and secular aspects of life, reflecting our shared need for meaning and connection. Whether through a wedding ceremony, a funeral, or a national celebration like New Year's Eve, rituals give shape to human experience, marking life's major transitions and anchoring us in the present moment. They also serve to connect us to the past, allowing us to honor traditions and reaffirm our place in the larger human story.

Rituals Mark Life's Transitions

Throughout life, people turn to rituals to mark significant transitions—birth, marriage, and death are perhaps the most universally recognized milestones. These rituals help individuals and communities acknowledge the changes in life's stages and offer a way to navigate the emotional and spiritual challenges that accompany them.

- Weddings: A wedding is a deeply symbolic ritual that celebrates the union of two individuals, often within the context of a larger community. Regardless of the specific religious or cultural practices involved, weddings are a celebration of love, commitment, and the creation of a new family. They serve not only to unite the couple but to bring together families and friends, reinforcing the bonds that connect individuals to their wider community. Through vows, blessings, and symbolic gestures, weddings are a ritualized acknowledgment of the power of love and partnership, reflecting the universal need for connection and belonging.
- Funerals: Funerals are perhaps the most poignant example of a ritual that helps individuals and communities come to terms with the profound mystery of death. They provide a space for

mourning, reflection, and healing, offering the living a way to honor the life of the deceased and confront the reality of loss. Across cultures, funeral rituals vary widely—some involve elaborate ceremonies, others are simple and intimate—but all serve the same fundamental purpose: to provide comfort and meaning in the face of death, and to reaffirm the continuity of life within the larger cycle of existence.

- Coming-of-Age Rituals: Many cultures have rituals that mark the transition from childhood to adulthood, such as bar mitzvahs, quinceañeras, or graduation ceremonies. These rites of passage celebrate personal growth and signify the individual's evolving role within the community. They help young people step into new phases of life with a sense of purpose and belonging, reminding them of the support and guidance available from their family, friends, and community.

Rituals Create a Sense of Community

Beyond their role in marking life's transitions, rituals foster a sense of community and shared identity. They bring people together in a shared experience, whether in joy or grief, celebration or reflection. In these moments, individuals feel connected not only to those around them but to the larger human story that transcends time and space. By participating in rituals, people affirm their place in the world and their connection to others, regardless of religious or cultural differences.

- Cultural and National Celebrations: Secular rituals, such as New Year's Eve, Independence Day, or Thanksgiving, offer opportunities for communities to come together and celebrate shared values, history, and aspirations. These rituals may not be explicitly religious, but they are deeply symbolic, representing collective hopes, gratitude, and unity. They offer a space for reflection on the past and for envisioning a future grounded in shared ideals.
- Communal Healing: In times of crisis or tragedy, rituals play an essential role in bringing communities together for healing and support. Memorial services, vigils, and moments of silence serve as collective expressions of grief, offering a way for people to process emotions and reaffirm their connection to one another. These rituals remind us that in times of hardship, we are not alone—we are

part of a larger community that shares in our pain and offers comfort.

The Sacred Within Secular Rituals

While many rituals are rooted in religious traditions, there are countless secular rituals that carry deep meaning and significance for individuals and communities. These rituals may not invoke specific deities or religious beliefs, but they still serve to connect people to something beyond themselves. Secular rituals can be profoundly sacred in their own way, offering a sense of reverence for life, for the earth, or for the human experience.

The Secular Sacred: Celebrations of Life

In modern society, secular rituals are often used to celebrate milestones such as birthdays, anniversaries, and achievements. These rituals provide opportunities to reflect on the passage of time, to honor personal growth, and to express gratitude for the people and experiences that shape our lives.

- Birthdays: A birthday is a simple yet powerful ritual that marks the passage of another year in a person's life. It is a time to celebrate life itself, to express gratitude for another year of experiences, and to honor the relationships that sustain us. Though secular in nature, birthdays are often filled with deep emotional and symbolic meaning, offering a moment of reflection on one's personal journey.

- Graduations and Achievements: Graduation ceremonies and other rituals that mark personal achievements serve as rites of passage, celebrating the individual's growth and perseverance. These moments of recognition, whether formal or informal, connect people to their communities by acknowledging the shared effort, support, and guidance that contributed to the individual's success.

Shared Rituals in the Digital Age

In today's interconnected world, digital platforms have become new spaces for rituals, allowing people to participate in communal experiences regardless of physical distance. Virtual ceremonies, live streamed events, and online memorials have emerged as modern rituals that unite people across the globe, offering a way to share in life's significant moments even when they cannot be together in person.

- Online Memorials: In the wake of the COVID-19 pandemic, virtual memorial services became a common way for families and communities to grieve together, even when separated by geography. These digital rituals serve the same purpose as traditional funerals—honoring the deceased, offering comfort to the bereaved, and reaffirming the bonds of community.
- Live Streamed Celebrations: Digital platforms have also allowed people to share in joyous occasions such as weddings, births, and milestone achievements. By creating spaces for virtual participation, these online rituals help people stay connected to one another and to the larger human experience, even when circumstances prevent them from gathering in person.

Rituals as Expressions of the Universal Need for Connection

At their core, rituals—whether religious or secular—reflect the universal human need to connect with something beyond ourselves. They allow us to express our deepest emotions, to honor life's transitions, and to participate in a shared human experience that transcends individual differences. Through rituals, we find meaning, comfort, and a sense of belonging in a world that is often uncertain and ever-changing.

The Role of Symbols in Rituals

Rituals are often filled with symbols—gestures, objects, and words that carry deep meaning. Whether it's the lighting of candles, the exchange of vows, or the breaking of bread, these symbols serve as reminders of the sacredness of life and our connection to the larger forces that shape it.

- Symbols of Love and Unity: In a wedding, the exchange of rings is a simple yet powerful symbol of love and commitment, representing the couple's union and their connection to a broader community. Similarly, in religious rituals, symbols such as the cross in Christianity or the chalice in Wiccan rituals serve as tangible reminders of the sacred, helping participants feel connected to the divine and to one another.
- Communal Participation: Many rituals invite communal participation through shared symbols,

such as lighting candles for peace or offering a toast during a celebration. These shared acts help to unite individuals in a common purpose, reinforcing the sense of community and belonging that lies at the heart of every ritual.

Conclusion: The Power of Rituals to Unite Us

Rituals are a fundamental part of human life, offering a way to connect with others, with ourselves, and with the larger forces that shape existence. Whether religious or secular, personal or communal, rituals serve as powerful expressions of the universal need for connection—to mark life's transitions, to celebrate love and joy, to mourn loss, and to reaffirm our place within the larger human story. Through rituals, we find a shared language that transcends differences in culture, religion, or belief, reminding us that we are all part of something greater.

Chapter 7: Bridging the Divide

Section 7.1: Overcoming Religious Conflict

Religious conflicts have been a source of division and violence throughout history, fueled by a belief in the superiority of one faith over another or by a misunderstanding of what different religions represent. Yet, at their core, most religious traditions emphasize love, compassion, and a sense of unity with all of creation. Religious conflicts often arise from a failure to recognize this shared foundation and the underlying unity that connects all spiritual traditions.

Drawing on the work of renowned scholar Karen Armstrong, particularly her writings on compassion, this section will explore how religious conflict stems from a misunderstanding of the fundamental unity beneath different beliefs and how embracing compassion can help foster dialogue and understanding between divided religious groups. Armstrong's emphasis on the Golden Rule—"treat others as you wish to be treated"—provides a powerful framework for transcending religious differences and building bridges between communities in conflict.

Religious Conflict and the Misunderstanding of Unity

At the heart of many religious conflicts is the belief that one's own faith holds the exclusive truth, while others are seen as false or misguided. This sense of exclusivity breeds mistrust, fear, and hostility toward those who hold different beliefs, often leading to violence and division. Yet, if we look more closely at the world's major religions, we find that most of them share similar ethical teachings and spiritual values. While the outer forms of religion—rituals, doctrines, and symbols—may differ, the inner essence of these traditions often speaks to the same core principles of love, compassion, and the search for meaning.

The Illusion of Separation

One of the primary causes of religious conflict is the illusion of separation—the belief that different religions are fundamentally opposed to one another. This misunderstanding often arises from a superficial reading of religious texts and traditions, which focuses on doctrinal differences rather than the shared ethical and spiritual principles that unite them. The result is a sense of otherness, where people of different faiths are seen as inherently different or even threatening.

- Doctrinal Rigidness: Many conflicts arise from the rigid interpretation of religious texts, where differences in language or practice are seen as insurmountable barriers. This rigidness prevents people from recognizing the shared goals of spiritual growth, compassion, and connection to the divine that are present in all religions.
- Cultural and Historical Factors: Often, religious conflicts are driven as much by cultural and political factors as by theology. Historical grievances, territorial disputes, and social inequality are frequently masked in religious terms, leading to the perception that the conflict is about faith when, in reality, it may be about power, identity, or resources.

Karen Armstrong: Compassion as the Key to Understanding

In her influential work, Karen Armstrong argues that the key to overcoming religious conflict lies in returning to the core ethical teachings of compassion found in all the world's religions. Armstrong's Charter for Compassion, launched in 2008, encourages people of all faiths—and those of no faith—to commit to the Golden Rule: treating others as we would wish to be treated. This simple yet profound principle, she argues, is a universal ethic that transcends religious divisions and can serve as a foundation for dialogue and mutual understanding.

The Universal Ethic of Compassion

Armstrong's work emphasizes that compassion is at the heart of all major religious traditions. Whether in Christianity's commandment to "love your neighbor as yourself," Islam's emphasis on mercy and justice, or Buddhism's cultivation of Metta (loving-kindness), compassion serves as the guiding principle for how human beings should relate to one another. By focusing on this shared value, Armstrong argues, we can begin to break down the barriers that divide religious communities and foster a greater sense of empathy and solidarity.

- The Golden Rule Across Traditions: The Golden Rule, found in various forms in nearly every religious tradition, encourages individuals to treat others with the same kindness, respect, and dignity they would want for themselves. This ethic of reciprocity can help bridge divides by shifting the focus from doctrinal differences to shared human values.

- Compassion as Action: Armstrong argues that compassion is not simply an emotion but a call to action. It requires actively working to alleviate the suffering of others, understanding their perspectives, and seeking justice in a way that honors their dignity and humanity. In this way, compassion can become a practical tool for addressing the root causes of religious conflict, whether through dialogue, peacemaking, or social justice initiatives.

Fostering Dialogue Between Divided Religious Groups

One of the most important ways to overcome religious conflict is to foster open dialogue between divided communities. Dialogue, when rooted in compassion and mutual respect, allows people to move beyond stereotypes and misunderstandings and begin to see one another as human beings with shared hopes, fears, and values. Armstrong's emphasis on compassionate listening encourages individuals to approach dialogue with an open heart and a willingness to learn from others.

- Listening with Compassion: Armstrong stresses that true dialogue requires active listening—not simply waiting for an opportunity to respond but genuinely trying to understand the other person's perspective. This kind of compassionate listening can help break down the walls of mistrust and hostility that often fuel religious conflict.
- Shared Rituals and Acts of Solidarity: Another way to foster understanding between divided religious groups is through shared rituals or acts of solidarity. Participating in each other's celebrations, prayers, or service projects can create a sense of unity and shared purpose, helping to build bridges between communities that may otherwise see themselves as fundamentally opposed.

The Path Toward Religious Reconciliation

While religious conflicts may seem intractable, history has shown that reconciliation is possible when people come together in a spirit of compassion, empathy, and understanding. By focusing on the common values that unite rather than the differences that divide, religious communities can begin to heal the wounds of conflict and work toward a more just and peaceful world.

Examples of Religious Reconciliation

Throughout history, there have been numerous examples of religious groups overcoming conflict and building lasting peace. These examples offer hope and inspiration for how compassion and dialogue can lead to reconciliation.

- South Africa's Truth and Reconciliation Commission: In the aftermath of apartheid, South Africa's Truth and Reconciliation Commission provided a platform for victims and perpetrators of violence to share their stories and seek forgiveness. The process, deeply influenced by religious and spiritual values, emphasized the importance of forgiveness, compassion, and restorative justice in healing a divided nation.
- Interfaith Initiatives in Northern Ireland: After decades of violence between Protestant and Catholic communities in Northern Ireland, interfaith initiatives have played a key role in fostering dialogue and understanding between the two groups. Programs that bring young people from

different religious backgrounds together to share their experiences and learn from one another have helped to break down stereotypes and build bridges between historically divided communities.

The Role of Compassion in Healing Religious Divides

Compassion is not only a tool for fostering dialogue but also a healing force that can mend the wounds of religious conflict. By cultivating compassion within ourselves and extending it to others, we create the conditions for reconciliation, forgiveness, and healing. Religious conflicts often leave deep scars—on individuals, families, and entire communities—but through compassion, those scars can begin to heal.

Forgiveness as a Path to Healing

Forgiveness is a central aspect of compassion, and it plays a critical role in healing the wounds of religious conflict. Forgiveness does not mean condoning or forgetting the harm that has been done, but rather, it is a way of releasing the anger, hatred, and desire for revenge that can perpetuate cycles of violence.

- Forgiveness in Christianity and Islam: Both Christianity and Islam emphasize the importance of forgiveness in building peace. In Christianity, Jesus teaches that forgiveness is essential for living a life of love and compassion, while Islam emphasizes the mercy of God and the importance of forgiving others as a reflection of divine mercy.
- The Power of Personal Forgiveness: In the context of religious conflict, personal acts of forgiveness can have profound effects. When individuals who have been harmed by religious violence choose to forgive their perpetrators, they create a ripple effect that can inspire others to follow their example, leading to broader communal healing.

Conclusion: Bridging the Divide Through Compassion and Understanding

Religious conflicts, while deeply rooted in history, culture, and theology, can be overcome by recognizing the fundamental unity that lies beneath different beliefs. By focusing on the shared values of compassion, forgiveness, and understanding, we can begin to bridge the divide between religious communities and foster a spirit of reconciliation. As Karen Armstrong reminds us, compassion is not just an emotion but a universal ethic—a call to action that can heal the wounds of division and create a more peaceful world.

By embracing compassion, engaging in dialogue, and recognizing humanity in one another, religious communities can move beyond conflict and toward a future of mutual respect, understanding, and peace.

Section 7.2: Finding Common Ground

In a world often divided by religious differences, the search for common ground becomes essential for fostering understanding and peace between communities. Interfaith dialogues and philosophical debates have played a significant role in revealing the shared ethical principles that unite diverse religious traditions. One of the most powerful examples of this shared moral foundation is the Golden Rule, which appears in almost every major religion. This principle of treating others as one would wish to be treated is a simple yet profound reminder of our shared humanity and the ethical responsibilities we hold toward one another.

In this section, we will explore how finding common ground through interfaith dialogue has helped to bridge divides between religious groups and created opportunities for cooperation, understanding, and mutual respect. By focusing on the shared values that transcend doctrinal differences, religious and philosophical communities can work together to address common challenges and promote peace.

The Golden Rule: A Universal Ethical Principle

The Golden Rule—"treat others as you wish to be treated"—is a universal ethical principle that can be found in almost every major religion, often considered the foundation of morality. Though expressed in different words, the underlying message is the same: we should extend to others the same kindness, respect, and dignity that we would want for ourselves. The widespread presence of the Golden Rule across diverse traditions highlights the deep-seated recognition of our interconnectedness and the shared moral obligations we have toward one another.

The Golden Rule Across Religions

The Golden Rule takes different forms in various religious texts, but its meaning remains consistent: compassion and empathy for others should guide our actions. This principle transcends cultural and theological boundaries, offering a common moral foundation for all human beings.

- Christianity: In the New Testament, Jesus teaches the Golden Rule as the central tenet of ethical behavior: *"So in everything, do to others what you would have them do to you, for this sums up the Law and the Prophets"* (Matthew 7:12). This passage underscores the importance of treating others with the same love and respect one would want in return.
- Islam: The Hadiths of the Prophet Muhammad contain similar teachings, emphasizing the importance of compassion and mutual respect: *"None of you truly believes until he loves for his brother what he loves for himself"* (Sahih al-Bukhari 13). This reflects the principle of empathy as a guiding force in human relationships.
- Judaism: In Leviticus, the Golden Rule is expressed as a commandment: *"Love your neighbor as yourself"* (Leviticus 19:18). This ethical principle is central to Jewish teachings on how individuals should treat

others, regardless of differences in background or belief.

- Hinduism: In Hinduism, the Golden Rule appears in the Mahabharata: *"This is the sum of duty: do not do to others what would cause pain if done to you."* This version emphasizes non-harm (ahimsa), a core value in Hindu ethics.

- Buddhism: The Dhammapada, a collection of sayings attributed to the Buddha, expresses a similar teaching: *"Treat not others in ways that you yourself would find hurtful."* The focus on empathy and compassion aligns with the broader Buddhist teachings on interconnectedness and the alleviation of suffering.

- Taoism: In Taoist thought, the principle of reciprocity is also central: *"Regard your neighbor's gain as your own gain, and your neighbor's loss as your own loss"* (T'ai Shang Kan Ying P'ien). This reflects the Taoist understanding of the interconnected nature of all things.

A Shared Moral Compass

The universality of the Golden Rule demonstrates that, at a fundamental level, all religious traditions recognize the importance of compassion, empathy, and justice in guiding human behavior. While the doctrinal specifics may differ, the ethical principle remains the same: we have a moral obligation to treat others with respect and care, just as we would hope to be treated in return. This shared moral compass serves as a powerful foundation for interfaith dialogue and cooperation.

Interfaith Dialogues: Discovering Common Principles

Interfaith dialogues provide a space for individuals from different religious traditions to come together, share their beliefs, and discover the common principles that unite them. These dialogues do not seek to erase the differences between religions but rather to celebrate diversity while focusing on shared values. Through open conversation, participants gain a deeper understanding of one another's faiths and begin to see that many of the ethical teachings in their traditions reflect the same underlying truths.

The Role of Interfaith Organizations

Organizations such as the Parliament of the World's Religions, United Religions Initiative, and local interfaith councils have played a crucial role in fostering dialogue and understanding between religious communities. These organizations often focus on common concerns—such as human rights, social justice, and environmental stewardship—that transcend individual belief systems. By emphasizing shared values, these groups help religious communities work together toward common goals, even when their theological beliefs may differ.

- The Parliament of the World's Religions: Since its founding in 1893, the Parliament of the World's Religions has served as a platform for interfaith dialogue and cooperation. At each of its gatherings, participants from diverse religious backgrounds come together to discuss pressing global issues, share spiritual practices, and explore the common ethical principles that unite their traditions.
- Interfaith Peacemaking: In regions affected by religious conflict, interfaith dialogue has proven to be a powerful tool for peacemaking. In areas such as the Middle East, India, and Africa, interfaith initiatives have helped to ease tensions by fostering understanding between communities. These dialogues often focus on shared values such as peace,

justice, and compassion, emphasizing the common humanity of all participants.

Philosophical Debates and Common Ground

In addition to religious dialogues, philosophical debates have played an important role in revealing the shared ethical foundations of various belief systems. Throughout history, philosophers and theologians from different traditions have engaged in debates about morality, the nature of truth, and the role of reason in spiritual life. While these debates often highlight important differences, they also reveal areas of agreement—particularly in relation to ethical principles.

- The Role of Reason and Ethics: Philosophical debates across cultures and religions often converge on questions of ethics. Thinkers from traditions as varied as Confucianism, Islamic philosophy, and Christian theology have all emphasized the importance of reason in guiding moral behavior. Despite doctrinal differences, many religious and philosophical traditions share the belief that reason and reflection can help individuals discern right from wrong and live in accordance with moral principles.

- The Search for Truth: Philosophers from different religious traditions have long engaged in a shared search for truth—whether through metaphysical inquiry, ethical reflection, or spiritual practice. This search often leads to the recognition of common truths about the nature of reality, the human condition, and the ethical responsibilities we have toward one another.

Finding Common Ground in Practice

While interfaith dialogues and philosophical debates help to reveal shared ethical principles, the true power of these shared values lies in their application. By focusing on common ground, religious and philosophical communities can work together to address some of the world's most pressing challenges, from poverty and inequality to environmental degradation and human rights violations. When religious groups come together to act on their shared values, they demonstrate the potential for unity, cooperation, and positive change.

Collaborative Social Justice Initiatives

One of the most powerful ways in which religious communities find common ground is through social justice initiatives. By focusing on shared concerns—such as helping the poor, protecting the environment, and promoting human dignity—religious groups can transcend doctrinal differences and work together to create a more just and compassionate world.

- Religious Coalition for Reproductive Choice: This interfaith organization brings together leaders from different religious traditions to advocate for reproductive rights and access to healthcare. By focusing on the shared values of justice, human dignity, and compassion, the coalition works to ensure that individuals have access to the services they need, regardless of their religious background.
- Interfaith Environmental Movements: In response to the growing threat of climate change, interfaith organizations have formed alliances to promote environmental stewardship. Groups like the Interfaith Power and Light movement bring together Christians, Jews, Muslims, Buddhists, and others to advocate for policies that protect the

environment and promote sustainable living. These initiatives emphasize the shared moral responsibility to care for the earth, a value present in many religious traditions.

Conclusion: Unity Through Shared Values

Despite the differences in doctrine, practice, and theology that exist between the world's religious traditions, there is a powerful common ground that unites them—an ethical foundation rooted in compassion, empathy, and the recognition of our shared humanity. The Golden Rule, present in almost every major religion, serves as a reminder that we all have a moral obligation to treat others with the same kindness, respect, and dignity that we would hope to receive.

Section 7.3: Toward a Global Ethic

In a world increasingly interconnected yet divided by religious, cultural, and political differences, the need for a global ethic—a set of shared moral principles that transcends individual traditions—has never been more pressing. One of the leading voices in this conversation is the Swiss theologian Hans Küng, who has long advocated for the development of a global ethic that draws upon the common values found in the world's major religions. Küng's vision calls for all faith traditions to recognize their shared moral responsibilities and to work together toward building a united and just global human community.

Küng's work emphasizes that while the world's religions may differ in theology and practice, they are united by core ethical principles that can serve as a foundation for peace, justice, and compassion on a global scale. His vision of a global ethic is rooted in the belief that cooperation among the world's religions is essential to addressing the most urgent challenges facing humanity, from poverty and inequality to environmental destruction and armed conflict. This section will explore Küng's vision of a global ethic, its foundational principles, and its potential to foster global unity and cooperation.

Hans Küng's Vision of a Global Ethic

Hans Küng's concept of a global ethic emerged from his decades of work as a Catholic theologian and advocate for interfaith dialogue. He first outlined this vision in his book

Global Responsibility: In Search of a New World Ethic, where he argued that the world's religions share a common ethical foundation that can serve as the basis for global cooperation. In 1993, at the Parliament of the World's Religions, Küng's vision was formalized in the Declaration Toward a Global Ethic, a document signed by religious leaders from various faiths that laid out the ethical principles that unite humanity.

At the heart of Küng's global ethic is the belief that no lasting peace between nations is possible without peace between religions, and that no peace between religions is possible without dialogue and cooperation. He argues that the major religious traditions must move beyond their doctrinal differences and work together to address the common ethical challenges facing humanity.

The Core Principles of a Global Ethic

Küng's global ethic is based on several core principles that he believes are shared across the world's religions. These principles emphasize human dignity, non-violence, justice, and compassion, and they provide a moral framework for building a peaceful and just global society.

1. The Principle of Humanity: At the center of Küng's global ethic is the recognition of the inherent dignity of every human being. This principle calls on all religions to respect the worth of every person, regardless of race, gender, nationality, or religious belief. By emphasizing the universal value of human life, this principle seeks to overcome the divisions that often arise from cultural and religious differences.

2. The Golden Rule: As in many interfaith dialogues, Küng highlights the Golden Rule as a universal moral principle that is present in all major religious traditions. The ethic of reciprocity—"treat others as you would like to be treated"—is a foundation for building harmonious relationships and fostering mutual respect between individuals and communities.

3. Commitment to Non-Violence and Justice: Küng's global ethic calls for a commitment to non-violence and justice. This principle challenges all religions to reject violence as a means of resolving conflict and to work toward creating a more just and equitable world. Küng emphasizes that religious communities have a responsibility to oppose violence in all its

forms—whether physical, structural, or cultural—and to advocate for the rights and dignity of the marginalized.

4. Commitment to Truth and Tolerance: Küng's vision also stresses the importance of truthfulness and tolerance. In a pluralistic world, where people of different cultures and faiths must coexist, it is essential that individuals are truthful in their dealings with one another and that they practice tolerance toward those with differing beliefs. By promoting dialogue, understanding, and openness, this principle seeks to reduce the misunderstandings and conflicts that often arise from religious and cultural differences.

5. Care for the Earth: Küng's global ethic also extends to the environment, calling for a commitment to environmental stewardship. The world's religions, Küng argues, share a moral obligation to protect the Earth and its ecosystems. This principle of care for the Earth is rooted in the understanding that humanity is not separate from nature but is part of a larger interconnected whole. By advocating for sustainable practices and respect for the

environment, Küng's global ethic seeks to address the ecological crises facing the planet.

Toward a United Human Community

Küng's vision of a global ethic is not simply a philosophical ideal; it is a call to action that challenges religious and cultural communities to work together toward building a united human community. This vision acknowledges the diversity of the world's religious traditions but insists that this diversity should not be a source of division. Instead, it should be seen as a source of strength, with each tradition contributing its unique insights to the collective effort to promote peace, justice, and human dignity.

Fostering Cooperation Between Religions

For Küng, a global ethic provides a common moral ground upon which the world's religions can cooperate in addressing global challenges. By focusing on shared ethical principles, religious communities can work together to address issues such as poverty, human rights, gender equality, and climate change. This cooperation is essential for creating a more just and sustainable world.

- Interfaith Collaboration for Social Justice: Many of the world's most pressing social issues—such as poverty, inequality, and human rights violations—can only be addressed through collaborative efforts that involve all sectors of society, including religious communities. By working together across religious and cultural lines, faith-based organizations can play a pivotal role in advocating for social justice and protecting the rights of vulnerable populations.
- Environmental Stewardship and Global Responsibility: Küng's emphasis on environmental stewardship reflects the growing recognition that the ecological crises facing the world require a global response. Religious communities, with their teachings on the sacredness of life and the interconnectedness of all beings, have an important role to play in promoting sustainable practices and advocating for policies that protect the environment. By embracing a global ethic that includes care for the Earth, religious traditions can help foster a sense of global responsibility and collective action.

Challenges and Opportunities

While Küng's vision of a global ethic offers a powerful framework for building a united human community, it also faces significant challenges. The diversity of religious beliefs, political interests, and cultural practices can sometimes make it difficult to find common ground. However, the growing recognition of shared global challenges—such as climate change, economic inequality, and geopolitical instability—has created new opportunities for cooperation.

- Overcoming Religious Exclusivism: One of the key challenges in realizing Küng's vision is the persistence of religious exclusivism, the belief that one's own religion is the only true path. This mindset can hinder interfaith cooperation and create barriers to dialogue. To overcome this challenge, religious leaders and communities must cultivate a spirit of openness and humility, recognizing that no single tradition holds all the answers to the world's problems.
- Building Global Solidarity: Küng's vision of a global ethic calls for the creation of a sense of global solidarity, where people from different cultures,

faiths, and backgrounds come together to address shared challenges. This requires not only dialogue but also practical efforts to promote peace, justice, and sustainability. By working together on concrete projects—whether in the fields of social justice, environmental protection, or human rights—religious communities can help to build a more united and compassionate global society.

A Global Ethic in Action

Küng's global ethic has already begun to influence religious and interfaith organizations around the world. The Parliament of the World's Religions, for example, has adopted Küng's Declaration Toward a Global Ethic as a guiding document for its work, encouraging religious leaders to promote the principles of compassion, justice, and non-violence. Similarly, many interfaith initiatives are now focusing on climate change, peacebuilding, and human rights, recognizing that these global challenges require a united response.

The Global Ethic and the Future

As the world becomes increasingly interconnected, the need for a global ethic will only grow more urgent. Küng's vision offers a hopeful path forward, one in which the world's religious traditions can play a central role in addressing the crises of our time. By embracing shared ethical principles and working together toward the common good, religious communities can help to build a world that is more just, compassionate, and sustainable for future generations.

Conclusion: The Moral Imperative of a Global Ethic

Hans Küng's vision of a global ethic calls on the world's religions to move beyond their differences and to recognize their shared moral responsibilities toward humanity and the planet. By focusing on universal principles—such as the Golden Rule, non-violence, justice, and care for the Earth—Küng offers a framework for creating a united human community, one that is capable of addressing the complex challenges of the modern world.

As we move forward, the adoption of a global ethic will be essential for fostering cooperation, promoting peace, and ensuring the well-being of future generations. By recognizing the common ethical foundations that unite us, we can work together to create a world that reflects the values of compassion, justice, and respect for all life.

Chapter 8: The Spiritual Insight of Oneness

Section 8.1: Mysticism and the Experience of Unity

Across the world's religious and spiritual traditions, mysticism offers a glimpse into a deeper reality—a reality in which the boundaries that ordinarily separate individuals from one another, from the divine, and from the cosmos dissolve. Mystical experiences are those rare moments in which individuals perceive the underlying unity of all things, transcending the ordinary limitations of time, space, and identity. These experiences reveal a profound oneness that connects all beings, leading the mystic to a direct experience of the ultimate reality that lies beyond ordinary perception.

Mystical traditions throughout history and across cultures have pointed to this same truth: that beneath the apparent diversity of the world, there is a fundamental unity that binds all of creation together. Whether through the Christian mysticism of Meister Eckhart, the poetic expressions of Jalaluddin Rumi, or the Buddhist realization of Nirvana, mystics have offered profound insights into the interconnectedness of life and the spiritual oneness that permeates the universe. In this section, we will explore how different mystical traditions from around the world point to the same experience of unity, offering a universal vision of spiritual oneness.

Meister Eckhart: The Unity of the Soul and God

One of the most influential Christian mystics, Meister Eckhart (1260–1328), taught that the soul and God are not separate but are united at their deepest level. For Eckhart, the ultimate goal of the spiritual life is to transcend the ego, letting go of the false sense of separation, and to realize the unity of the soul with the divine. His mystical teachings emphasize that the divine presence is not something external or distant but is within each individual, and by looking inward, one can experience union with God.

The Birth of God in the Soul

A central theme in Eckhart's mysticism is the idea of the birth of God in the soul. He taught that, in the depths of the human soul, there is a divine spark—an aspect of the soul that is directly connected to God. Through contemplation and inner stillness, this divine spark can be awakened, allowing the individual to experience the birth of God within themselves.

- Ego Dissolution: Eckhart emphasized the importance of letting go of the ego in order to experience the unity of the soul with God. He often spoke of Gelassenheit, or "letting go," as the process of surrendering one's individual will and desires to align with the divine will. In doing so, the individual becomes one with God, experiencing the oneness that underlies all existence.
- Unity with the Divine: For Eckhart, the ultimate mystical insight is the realization that there is no true separation between the soul and God. He famously said, *"The eye with which I see God is the same eye with which God sees me."* This statement reflects Eckhart's belief that, at the deepest level, there is only one consciousness—one unified reality—and that the distinction between God and the soul is illusory.

Jalaluddin Rumi: Love as the Force of Unity

The 13th-century Persian poet and Sufi mystic Jalaluddin Rumi (1207–1273) is one of the most celebrated mystics in the world. In his poetry, Rumi speaks of love as the driving force behind the universe, a force that unites all beings and draws the soul back to its divine source. For Rumi, the experience of mystical love reveals the oneness of all existence, dissolving the boundaries between self and other, lover and beloved, human and divine.

The Journey of the Soul to the Beloved

In Rumi's mystical vision, the soul is on a journey to return to its Beloved—a metaphor for God or the ultimate reality. This journey is driven by love, which Rumi describes as the force of unity that connects all things. Through love, the soul is drawn closer to the divine, eventually realizing that it was never truly separate from the Beloved in the first place.

- Love as a Path to Oneness: For Rumi, love is not merely an emotional experience but a metaphysical principle that binds all of creation together. In one of his famous verses, he writes, *"The minute I heard my first love story, I started looking for you, not knowing how blind that was. Lovers don't finally meet somewhere. They're in each other all along."* This line speaks to the mystical insight that the soul and the Beloved are not separate—they are already one, and the journey of love is simply the realization of this truth.

- Union with the Divine: The goal of the mystical path, according to Rumi, is fana—the annihilation of the ego in the love of God. Through this process of surrender, the soul transcends its individual identity and becomes one with the divine. In his poetry, Rumi frequently describes the experience of union with God as a state of ecstasy and joy, where all distinctions between self and other dissolve, and the soul is absorbed into the infinite oneness of the divine.

Buddhist Nirvana: The Realization of Interconnectedness

In the Buddhist tradition, the mystical experience of Nirvana represents the ultimate realization of interconnectedness and the dissolution of the ego. Nirvana is not a place or a state of existence but the cessation of suffering and the liberation from the illusion of separateness. According to the Buddha's teachings, the root of human suffering lies in the belief that the self is separate from others and from the world. Nirvana is the direct experience of the truth that all beings are interconnected, and that there is no permanent, independent self.

Dependent Origination: The Web of Interconnectedness

A key concept in Buddhist philosophy is dependent origination (Pratītyasamutpāda), which teaches that all things arise in dependence on other things. Nothing exists in isolation; everything is interconnected, and all phenomena are interdependent. This insight forms the basis of the Buddhist understanding of no-self (Anatta), the realization that the self is not a fixed, separate entity but is always in relation to everything else.

- Ego Dissolution in Meditation: In Buddhist meditation practices, such as Vipassana or Zen, practitioners cultivate mindfulness and insight into the nature of reality. As they observe the impermanence and interdependence of all things, they come to understand that the ego is an illusion. This dissolution of the ego leads to a profound sense of oneness with the world, where the distinction

between self and other fades away, and the practitioner experiences the interconnectedness of all life.
- Nirvana as the Experience of Unity: The experience of Nirvana is often described as a state of profound peace and liberation, where the suffering caused by attachment to the ego is transcended. In Nirvana, the individual realizes that they are not separate from the world but are part of the flow of existence. This realization of oneness with all things is the ultimate goal of the Buddhist path.

The Universal Truth of Mystical Unity

While the language and symbols used by mystics vary across different religious traditions, the underlying insight remains the same: that all things are one, and that the boundaries we perceive between self and other, human and divine, are ultimately illusory. Whether through the Christian mysticism of Meister Eckhart, the Sufi teachings of Rumi, or the Buddhist realization of Nirvana, mystics have consistently pointed to the truth of oneness—a truth that transcends individual traditions and offers a universal vision of spiritual unity.

Common Themes in Mystical Traditions

- Ego Dissolution: A common theme in mystical traditions is the dissolution of the ego, the false sense of self that separates the individual from others and from the divine. Whether through contemplation, meditation, or love, mystics teach that the ego must be surrendered in order to experience unity with the ultimate reality.
- Union with the Divine: Mystical experiences often involve a sense of union with the divine or the cosmos. In this state of union, the individual no longer perceives themselves as separate from the rest of creation but recognizes their oneness with all that is.
- Interconnectedness: Mystics across traditions emphasize the interconnectedness of all life. This insight reveals that all beings are part of a larger whole, and that the apparent divisions between people, nature, and the divine are illusions. In this sense, mystical experiences offer a vision of a world

in which everything is deeply interconnected and interdependent.

Conclusion: Mysticism as a Path to Oneness

Mystical experiences offer a direct and transformative insight into the oneness that underlies all of existence. Whether through the Christian mysticism of Meister Eckhart, the Sufi teachings of Rumi, or the Buddhist realization of Nirvana, mystics across cultures and traditions have pointed to the same profound truth: that we are all connected, and that the divisions we perceive between ourselves and the world are illusions. By dissolving the ego and experiencing the unity of all things, mystics offer a powerful vision of spiritual oneness—a vision that transcends religious boundaries and invites all people to recognize their shared connection to the divine and to one another.

Section 8.2: The Self and the Whole

At the heart of many spiritual teachings is the notion that true enlightenment or awakening involves the dissolution of the individual ego or self, leading to an experience of unity with the whole of existence. One of the most profound voices in modern spiritual thought on this topic is the Indian philosopher and teacher Jiddu Krishnamurti (1895–1986). Krishnamurti challenged conventional understandings of spirituality and enlightenment, arguing that the key to spiritual freedom is the dissolution of the self—not through religious belief or tradition, but through a direct perception of reality as it is.

Krishnamurti's teachings emphasize that personal enlightenment involves recognizing that the self, as we typically understand it, is a construct of thought—a bundle of conditioned responses, memories, and attachments. When we realize the illusory nature of the self, we can begin to experience our true place within the greater scheme of existence. In this section, we explore Krishnamurti's teachings on the self, the illusion of separateness, and how dissolving the self leads to a state of oneness with the whole.

Jiddu Krishnamurti: The Illusion of the Self

Krishnamurti's core teaching revolves around the idea that the self, or the ego, is a product of thought and conditioning. He believed that human beings are trapped in patterns of thought and behavior that reinforce the illusion of a separate, individual self. This illusion creates a sense of isolation and division, not only between people but also between the individual and the world.

The Conditioned Self

Krishnamurti argued that the self is a result of conditioning—the accumulation of experiences, beliefs, desires, fears, and societal influences that shape our identities. From an early age, we are taught to see ourselves as separate entities, defined by our thoughts, achievements, relationships, and cultural roles. This conditioned sense of self leads to conflict, anxiety, and suffering because it creates an artificial boundary between "me" and "the world."

- Thought as the Root of Division: According to Krishnamurti, thought is responsible for creating the divisions that separate us from the rest of existence. Thought is based on past experiences and knowledge, and while it is necessary for practical purposes, it also perpetuates the illusion of a fixed, separate self. Krishnamurti taught that as long as we identify with our thoughts and the conditioned mind, we remain trapped in a cycle of fear, desire, and conflict.

- **The False Self:** Krishnamurti emphasized that the self we identify with is not real in any absolute sense—it is a construct, a psychological illusion. This false self is constantly seeking security, recognition, and fulfillment, but it is never satisfied because it is rooted in a sense of lack and separation. True freedom, according to Krishnamurti, can only be found when we see through the illusion of the self and recognize that we are not separate from the world around us.

Dissolution of the Self and the Experience of Wholeness

For Krishnamurti, enlightenment or awakening is not something to be achieved through effort or discipline. It is not the result of following a particular spiritual path or adopting specific practices. Instead, it is the spontaneous realization that the self is an illusion and that we are already part of the whole—the totality of existence. This realization brings about a radical shift in consciousness, where the sense of separation dissolves, and one experiences a state of oneness with life.

Observing Without Judgment

Krishnamurti taught that the dissolution of the self can only occur through pure observation—the ability to observe one's thoughts, emotions, and actions without judgment, interpretation, or interference. He called this process choiceless awareness or pure awareness. When we observe the workings of the mind without trying to change or control them, we begin to see that the self is simply a series of conditioned responses. In this state of awareness, the illusion of separateness fades away, revealing the underlying unity of all things.

- Freedom from the Known: Krishnamurti often spoke of the need to be free from the known—free from the past, from conditioned thought, and from the psychological structures that define the self. When we are no longer bound by the known, we can perceive life in its wholeness, without the filters of memory and belief. This direct perception allows us to experience reality as it is, free from the distortions of the ego.

- The State of Wholeness: In the state of wholeness that arises from the dissolution of the self, there is no longer a sense of "I" as separate from the world. Krishnamurti described this state as one of total integration, where the individual is no longer in conflict with themselves or with others. In this state, one is deeply connected to the flow of life, experiencing a profound sense of unity with the universe.

Recognizing One's Place in the Greater Scheme of Existence

Krishnamurti's teachings suggest that enlightenment involves recognizing one's true place within the greater scheme of existence. This recognition is not a matter of intellectual understanding but of direct, experiential realization. When the illusion of the separate self dissolves, what remains is a sense of belonging to the whole of life—a realization that we are not isolated individuals but integral parts of the totality of existence.

Interconnectedness and the Whole

Krishnamurti taught that when we are no longer identified with the ego, we can see that life is interconnected and that there is no division between the self and the whole. This realization brings about a deep sense of compassion and responsibility for all living beings. In recognizing our place in the greater scheme of existence, we understand that our actions, thoughts, and choices are not isolated—they affect the whole.

- Living in Harmony with the Whole: When we see ourselves as part of the whole, we naturally begin to live in harmony with life. Krishnamurti emphasized that true morality arises from this sense of interconnectedness, not from adherence to rules or doctrines. In this state, we act out of love and compassion, not out of fear or desire. Our actions are aligned with the flow of life, and we no longer contribute to conflict or division.

The End of Conflict

The dissolution of the self also leads to the end of conflict, both within the individual and in the world. Krishnamurti taught that all forms of conflict—whether personal, interpersonal, or global—stem from the illusion of separateness. When we see ourselves as separate from others, we become attached to our own desires, beliefs, and fears, leading to conflict and division. However, when we realize that we are part of the whole, conflict becomes unnecessary, and we begin to act in ways that promote harmony and unity.

The Universal Insight of Oneness

Krishnamurti's teachings on the dissolution of the self are deeply aligned with the mystical traditions of oneness found in many religions and philosophies. Like the Buddhist concept of Anatta (no-self) and the Advaita Vedanta teaching of non-duality, Krishnamurti's insight points to the ultimate truth that the self is an illusion and that enlightenment involves recognizing our oneness with the totality of existence.

Common Themes in Mystical Traditions

- Ego Dissolution: Mystical traditions across the world emphasize the dissolution of the ego as the key to spiritual awakening. Krishnamurti's teachings echo this insight, showing that when the false sense of self dissolves, we can experience the unity of all things.

- Direct Perception: Krishnamurti's emphasis on direct, choiceless awareness is similar to the meditative practices of Zen Buddhism and Advaita Vedanta, where practitioners cultivate a direct perception of reality without interference from the conditioned mind. This direct perception reveals the underlying oneness of life.

- Compassion and Responsibility: The realization of oneness leads to a deep sense of compassion and responsibility for others, as we come to understand that our well-being is intertwined with the well-being of all beings. This insight is shared by mystical traditions around the world, which teach that love and compassion naturally arise from the experience of unity.

Conclusion: Enlightenment as Unity with the Whole

Jiddu Krishnamurti's teachings on the dissolution of the self offer a profound vision of enlightenment as the realization of one's oneness with the whole of existence. By seeing through the illusion of the separate self, we can experience the interconnectedness of life and recognize our true place in the greater scheme of things. This realization brings about a state of wholeness, where conflict and division give way to harmony, compassion, and a deep sense of belonging.

In dissolving the boundaries that separate us from one another and from the world, we come to see that we are not isolated individuals but integral parts of the universe. This insight offers a path to personal enlightenment, as well as a vision of a more compassionate and interconnected world.

Section 8.3: Science Meets Mysticism

In recent decades, modern science has made discoveries that resonate profoundly with ancient mystical teachings. While science and spirituality are often seen as separate or even opposing worldviews, certain fields of scientific inquiry—especially quantum mechanics and cosmology—are increasingly revealing truths about the nature of reality that mirror the insights of mystics throughout history. These discoveries suggest that at the deepest levels, everything in the universe is fundamentally interconnected, a concept central to both mysticism and modern physics.

One of the most influential works in bridging the gap between science and mysticism is Fritjof Capra's *The Tao of Physics*. Capra argues that the discoveries of modern physics, particularly quantum mechanics, echo ancient spiritual philosophies, especially those found in Taoism, Buddhism, and Hinduism. He suggests that both science and mysticism point toward the same ultimate truth: the oneness of all things.

In this section, we will explore how modern science, through quantum theory and other groundbreaking discoveries, aligns with the mystical concept of interconnectedness, emphasizing that both science and spirituality point to a unified vision of reality.

Quantum Mechanics: The Interconnectedness of All Things

Quantum mechanics is one of the most significant scientific developments of the 20th century, revolutionizing our understanding of the physical world. Unlike classical physics, which views objects as distinct and separate, quantum mechanics reveals that particles at the subatomic level are not independent entities but are deeply interconnected with one another. This interconnectedness is often referred to as quantum entanglement, where particles that have interacted with one another remain linked, even when separated by vast distances. Changes in one particle can instantly affect the other, regardless of the distance between them.

The Breakdown of Separateness in Quantum Physics

One of the key insights of quantum mechanics is that the classical idea of separateness is an illusion. At the quantum level, particles do not behave like isolated objects but as parts of a larger, interconnected whole. The famous double-slit experiment, for example, demonstrated that the behavior of particles can change depending on whether they are being observed, suggesting that the observer and the observed are fundamentally linked. This challenges the traditional notion of objective reality, where the observer is separate from what is being observed.

- Wave-Particle Duality: Another important concept in quantum mechanics is wave-particle duality, which reveals that particles can behave both as discrete particles and as waves, depending on how they are measured. This duality highlights the fluid, interconnected nature of reality at the quantum level. The idea that particles are both individual and part of a larger wave system mirrors the mystical insight that the self is both distinct and one with the whole.

- Non-Locality and Entanglement: Quantum entanglement, often referred to as "spooky action at a distance," demonstrates that particles are not truly separate from one another but remain connected, regardless of physical distance. This phenomenon suggests that at the most fundamental level, reality is not made up of isolated objects but is a web of interconnected relationships. This mirrors the mystical insight that all things in the universe are interconnected and interdependent.

Fritjof Capra and The Tao of Physics

In his groundbreaking book *The Tao of Physics*, Fritjof Capra draws parallels between the findings of quantum mechanics and the philosophical insights of Eastern mysticism, particularly Taoism, Buddhism, and Hinduism. Capra argues that the discoveries of modern physics, particularly the ideas of interconnectedness and the fluid nature of reality, echo the teachings of ancient mystics who recognized the oneness of all things.

The Tao and Quantum Mechanics

Capra points out that in Taoism, the universe is seen as a dynamic and interconnected whole, in which everything is in a constant state of flux. The Tao, which means "the way," represents the underlying unity of the cosmos. This concept is strikingly similar to the discoveries of quantum mechanics, where particles are understood not as isolated objects but as part of a continuous, ever-changing field of energy.

- The Dance of the Universe: In *The Tao of Physics*, Capra describes the behavior of particles in quantum mechanics as a "cosmic dance," in which particles are not fixed entities but patterns of energy that interact with one another in an intricate web of relationships. This view aligns with the Taoist understanding of reality as a harmonious,

interconnected process, where all things are in constant motion and transformation.
- Beyond Duality: One of the key insights of both quantum mechanics and Eastern mysticism is the rejection of duality. In quantum mechanics, the distinction between particle and wave, or between matter and energy, breaks down. Similarly, in Taoism and Buddhism, dualities such as self and other, or subject and object, are seen as illusions. Both perspectives point to the idea that reality is a unified whole, where apparent distinctions are temporary and relative.

The Buddhist Concept of Interdependence

Capra also draws connections between quantum physics and the Buddhist concept of interdependent origination (Pratītyasamutpāda), which teaches that all phenomena arise in dependence on other phenomena. Nothing exists in isolation; everything is part of a vast network of causes and conditions. This idea aligns closely with the insights of quantum mechanics, which show that particles are not independent entities but exist in relation to other particles and forces.

- The Illusion of the Independent Self: In Buddhism, the notion of Anatta (no-self) teaches that the self is not a fixed, independent entity but is instead a collection of constantly changing processes. This is similar to the idea in quantum mechanics that particles do not have a fixed, independent existence but are part of an interconnected field of energy. Both teachings suggest that separateness is an illusion and that the true nature of reality is one of interconnectedness.

Cosmology and the Unified Field

Beyond quantum mechanics, modern cosmology has also contributed to the scientific understanding of the interconnectedness of the universe. The idea of a unified field, which seeks to explain how all forces in the universe are part of a single, cohesive framework, echoes mystical ideas of oneness. Albert Einstein's work on relativity and the quest for a unified theory of everything are part of this scientific effort to understand the underlying unity of the cosmos.

The Big Bang and the Origins of Oneness

Modern cosmology tells us that the universe began as a single point of energy in the Big Bang. From this initial singularity, the entire universe expanded, creating the stars, galaxies, and planets. This scientific narrative parallels mystical teachings that suggest all of creation emerges from a single source. Whether seen through the lens of the Tao, Brahman in Hinduism, or the Oneness of Allah in Sufism, the idea that all of existence comes from a unified source is central to both mysticism and modern cosmology.

- The Unity of Matter and Energy: Einstein's famous equation, $E=mc^2$, reveals that matter and energy are interchangeable. This insight breaks down the classical distinction between solid matter and invisible energy, suggesting that everything in the universe is a manifestation of the same underlying reality. This concept aligns with mystical teachings that see the material world as a reflection or manifestation of a deeper spiritual reality.
- The Search for a Unified Theory: Scientists today continue to search for a unified theory of everything, which would reconcile the forces of gravity, electromagnetism, and quantum mechanics into a single framework. This search mirrors the mystical

quest to understand the oneness of all things. Just as mystics seek to transcend the illusion of separateness and experience the unity of existence, physicists seek to uncover the fundamental unity that underlies the diverse phenomena of the physical world.

Science and Mysticism: Different Paths, Same Destination

While science and mysticism approach reality from different perspectives, both offer profound insights into the oneness and interconnectedness of all things. Science uses empirical observation and experimentation to reveal the underlying patterns and forces that shape the universe, while mysticism offers a direct, experiential realization of the unity of existence. Despite their differences, both paths ultimately point to the same truth: that the divisions we perceive in the world—between self and other, matter and energy, subject and object—are illusions, and that all things are part of a single, interconnected whole.

The Complementary Nature of Science and Mysticism

Capra and other thinkers suggest that science and mysticism are not opposed but are complementary ways of understanding reality. While science focuses on the external, measurable aspects of the universe, mysticism explores the inner, subjective experience of oneness. Both approaches are necessary for a complete understanding of the nature of existence.

- Mystical Experience and Scientific Insight: Mystical experiences often reveal truths about the interconnectedness of life that are later confirmed by scientific discoveries. For example, the mystical insight that all beings are interconnected aligns with the scientific understanding of quantum entanglement and the interdependence of ecosystems. Both science and mysticism offer a vision of a world where everything is connected, and where the boundaries between self and other are fluid and permeable.

Chapter 9: Living a Connected Life

Section 9.1: Spirituality in Everyday Life

The profound realization of oneness—the interconnectedness of all life—need not remain an abstract concept confined to mystical experiences or philosophical inquiry. Instead, this insight can be lived out in our daily lives, influencing our actions, choices, and relationships. By aligning our everyday lives with the understanding of interconnectedness, we can cultivate a way of living that reflects the unity of all things, fostering greater compassion, mindfulness, and harmony in our personal and communal lives.

The American transcendentalist philosopher Henry David Thoreau offers an inspiring model for this kind of life through his idea of living deliberately. In his famous work *Walden*, Thoreau advocates for a life lived with intention and in harmony with nature, where one's actions are guided by a deep awareness of the world's interconnectedness. This approach to life invites us to integrate spiritual insights into the rhythms of daily living, making spirituality not just a set of beliefs but a way of being.

Living Oneness Through Compassion

One of the most immediate ways to bring the understanding of oneness into everyday life is through compassion. When we recognize that we are all interconnected—that the well-being of others is inseparable from our own—we are naturally moved to act with kindness and empathy. Compassion becomes not just an emotional response but a moral imperative grounded in the understanding that, at the deepest level, we are all part of the same whole.

Compassion as a Practice

Living compassionately involves making deliberate choices to ease the suffering of others and to contribute positively to the lives of those around us. Whether through small acts of kindness or larger commitments to service, compassion allows us to embody the spiritual insight of oneness in a tangible way.

- Acts of Kindness: Simple actions, such as offering help to someone in need, listening to a friend with full attention, or practicing patience in difficult situations, can reflect the understanding that we are all interconnected. These small gestures, when performed with awareness, contribute to the well-being of others and strengthen the sense of unity in our relationships and communities.

- Compassionate Service: Many people extend their sense of connectedness through involvement in community service or humanitarian efforts. Whether volunteering at a local shelter, working toward social justice, or participating in environmental initiatives, acts of service can help us live out the principle of oneness by contributing to the greater good. By focusing on the needs of others, we dissolve the boundaries between self and other, recognizing that we are all part of the same human family.

Mindfulness and Presence in Everyday Life

Another way to live out the spiritual insight of oneness is through mindfulness—the practice of being fully present and aware in each moment. Mindfulness helps us to cultivate a deeper connection to ourselves, to others, and to the world around us. When we approach life with mindfulness, we are more likely to experience the interconnectedness of all things directly, as we become attuned to the subtle ways in which our actions, thoughts, and feelings ripple through the web of life.

Mindful Living

Living mindfully means paying attention to the present moment without judgment, allowing us to respond to life with greater clarity, openness, and compassion. Mindfulness can transform even the most ordinary activities into opportunities for spiritual growth, helping us to see the sacredness in everyday life.

- Mindful Awareness: Practicing mindfulness in daily activities—such as walking, eating, or speaking—helps us stay grounded in the present moment and recognize the beauty of interconnectedness in all things. For example, when we eat mindfully, we can reflect on the many people, animals, and natural forces that contributed to the food on our plate, cultivating a sense of gratitude for the larger web of life that sustains us.
- Responding Rather Than Reacting: Mindfulness allows us to respond to situations with awareness

rather than reacting out of habit or conditioning. By creating space for thoughtful reflection, we can make choices that align with the values of interconnectedness and compassion. For instance, when faced with conflict, mindfulness helps us step back, consider the larger picture, and act in ways that promote harmony and understanding rather than division.

Building Communities of Connection

A third way to live out the insight of oneness is through community building. Humans are inherently social beings, and our relationships with others are one of the most direct ways we experience interconnectedness. By creating communities that reflect the values of compassion, cooperation, and mutual support, we can help foster a sense of unity that transcends individualism and promotes collective well-being.

Creating Spaces for Connection

Communities that emphasize inclusivity, mutual respect, and shared responsibility allow individuals to feel connected not only to one another but also to the larger whole. These communities can take many forms, from families and neighborhoods to spiritual or activist groups, but all share the common goal of supporting each member's growth and well-being.

- Collaborative Efforts: Building a connected community often involves collaboration and shared efforts toward common goals. Whether organizing a neighborhood cleanup, hosting community meals, or engaging in collective activism, working together strengthens bonds and reflects the interconnectedness of all participants. In these shared experiences, we can see how our individual actions contribute to the collective good.
- Supporting Each Other's Growth: In a community rooted in oneness, members are encouraged to support one another's personal and spiritual growth. This might involve offering emotional or practical support, sharing knowledge, or simply being present for one another during times of difficulty. By fostering an environment where people feel seen, heard, and valued, communities can become

powerful expressions of interconnectedness and compassion.

Thoreau's Vision of Living Deliberately

The 19th-century transcendentalist Henry David Thoreau offers a timeless vision of how to live a connected life through his philosophy of living deliberately. In his seminal work *Walden*, Thoreau advocates for a life of simplicity, intentionality, and deep connection to nature. He believed that by living deliberately—by consciously choosing how we spend our time and attention—we can experience a profound sense of harmony with the natural world and with ourselves.

Simplicity and Intentionality

For Thoreau, living deliberately meant stripping away the distractions and excesses of modern life in order to focus on what truly matters. He saw simplicity as a path to clarity and connection, where one's energy is directed toward meaningful pursuits rather than scattered among superficial concerns.

- Living with Purpose: Thoreau's philosophy invites us to ask, "What is most important to me, and how can I live in alignment with that?" By living with purpose and clarity, we can ensure that our actions are consistent with our values and that we are contributing to the greater whole in meaningful ways.

- Harmony with Nature: Thoreau believed that living in harmony with nature was essential to living a connected life. In *Walden*, he describes his experience of immersing himself in the natural world, where he discovered a deep sense of interconnectedness with the environment and all living things. This harmony with nature is a reminder that we are not separate from the earth but are part of its intricate web of life. By cultivating a relationship with nature—whether through time spent outdoors, sustainable living practices, or environmental activism—we can deepen our understanding of oneness and live in a way that honors our connection to the planet.

Spirituality as a Way of Being

Ultimately, living a connected life means approaching each day with an awareness of our interconnectedness with others, with nature, and with the universe. Spirituality, in this sense, is not confined to specific practices or beliefs but is a way of being in the world—a way of moving through life with mindfulness, compassion, and a deep respect for the unity that underlies all existence.

By integrating the insights of oneness into our daily lives—through acts of kindness, mindful awareness, community building, and a deliberate approach to living—we can transform spirituality from a distant concept into a lived reality. In doing so, we honor the truth of interconnectedness and contribute to a more harmonious, compassionate world.

Section 9.2: Ethical Living and the Global Community

The recognition of our fundamental interconnectedness with all life does not remain purely a spiritual or philosophical insight; it has profound implications for how we live ethically in the world. By understanding that we are part of a global community—connected to people, animals, and the environment—we are called to make choices that reflect this awareness of unity. Ethical living, then, becomes about caring for others as extensions of ourselves and for the planet as the very ecosystem that sustains us all.

One of the leading voices in modern ethical philosophy is Peter Singer, whose work on effective altruism challenges us to live in ways that maximize the positive impact we have on the global community. Singer's approach calls for an ethical consideration that goes beyond our immediate surroundings, encouraging us to take into account the welfare of people around the world, as well as future generations and non-human animals. By making deliberate choices that are informed by our interconnectedness, we can contribute to a more just and sustainable global society.

Ethical Living as an Expression of Oneness

At the heart of ethical living is the recognition that our actions affect not only ourselves but also the wider world. Every choice we make, from how we treat others to how we consume resources, ripples out into the global community and the environment. Living ethically means acknowledging this interconnectedness and striving to minimize harm while maximizing well-being for all beings.

How We Treat Others

Ethical living begins with how we treat the people around us. When we recognize that each person is part of the larger web of life, our actions toward others become an expression of compassion and solidarity. This includes not only those in our immediate circle but also people in distant parts of the world who may be affected by our choices, such as the workers who produce the goods we consume or the communities impacted by environmental degradation.

- Global Responsibility: Ethical living calls for us to take responsibility for the well-being of others, even those we may never meet. The idea of global responsibility suggests that we should extend our circle of concern to include people across the world, especially those who are vulnerable or living in poverty. By recognizing our shared humanity, we can make choices that contribute to the global good, whether through conscious consumption, philanthropy, or advocating for human rights.
- Everyday Acts of Kindness: While global responsibility is important, ethical living also manifests in our everyday interactions with others.

Simple acts of kindness, such as treating others with respect, listening with empathy, and offering help where needed, reflect the understanding that we are all interconnected. These small gestures create a ripple effect of compassion that strengthens the bonds between individuals and communities.

Caring for the Planet

The insight of interconnectedness also extends to how we treat the natural world. The Earth is not a separate entity that we can exploit without consequence; it is the very source of our sustenance, and we are part of its intricate ecosystems. Ethical living, therefore, requires us to care for the planet in ways that ensure its health and sustainability for future generations.

Sustainable Living

One of the most direct ways we can live ethically in relation to the planet is through sustainable living—making choices that reduce our environmental impact and conserve natural resources. This includes everything from reducing waste and conserving energy to supporting renewable energy sources and adopting more sustainable diets.

- Conscious Consumption: Ethical living calls for us to be mindful of the impact our consumption has on the environment. This might mean choosing products that are ethically sourced, reducing single-use plastics, or buying locally to minimize the carbon footprint of transportation. By making these choices, we contribute to the well-being of the planet and the global community.
- Environmental Activism: Beyond individual choices, many people extend their ethical living to include environmental activism. This might involve participating in community efforts to clean up local ecosystems, advocating for policies that address climate change, or supporting organizations that work to protect biodiversity. Environmental activism is a way of living out the understanding that the health of the planet is inextricably linked to the well-being of all life.

One of the most compelling frameworks for ethical living in a global context comes from Peter Singer and his philosophy of effective altruism. Singer argues that we have a moral obligation to use our resources in ways that do the most good, especially when it comes to alleviating global poverty and suffering. Effective altruism is about maximizing the positive impact of our actions, ensuring that we are contributing to the greatest good for the greatest number of people.

The Moral Imperative of Altruism

Singer's philosophy is grounded in the belief that all lives are of equal moral worth, regardless of where someone lives or their proximity to us. He argues that, in an interconnected world, we cannot ignore the suffering of people in distant countries simply because they are not physically close to us. Instead, we should take action to alleviate suffering wherever it occurs.

- Alleviating Global Poverty: A central focus of Singer's work is on addressing global poverty. He argues that those of us who are financially comfortable have a moral obligation to help those who are living in extreme poverty, especially when a relatively small amount of money can have a significant impact on their lives. Effective altruism encourages us to donate to charities and organizations that have a proven track record of making the greatest positive impact, such as providing clean water, basic healthcare, or education in impoverished regions.

- Maximizing Impact: The principle of effective altruism is about not just doing good, but doing the most good with the resources we have. Singer encourages individuals to carefully evaluate where their time, money, and efforts can have the greatest positive effect. This often means supporting evidence-based interventions that address the root causes of suffering or that provide the most cost-effective solutions to pressing global problems.

Ethical Consideration of Animals

In addition to his work on global poverty, Singer is also a leading advocate for the ethical treatment of animals. He argues that the suffering of non-human animals should be given equal consideration to that of humans, as they are capable of experiencing pain and suffering in much the same way. This insight is an extension of the principle of interconnectedness, recognizing that our moral concern should not stop at the boundaries of our own species.

- Reducing Harm to Animals: Ethical living, according to Singer, involves making choices that reduce harm to animals, whether through adopting a plant-based diet, supporting animal welfare organizations, or advocating for laws that protect animals from cruelty and exploitation. By extending our compassion to all sentient beings, we can live in a way that reflects the oneness of all life.

Ethical Choices in a Globalized World

In today's globalized world, our actions have far-reaching consequences that extend beyond our immediate environment. The choices we make—whether in how we consume, how we vote, or how we engage with the world—impact not only our own lives but also the lives of people around the world and the health of the planet. Ethical living, therefore, requires us to take a global perspective, considering the long-term effects of our actions on future generations, on vulnerable populations, and on the Earth itself.

Thinking Globally, Acting Locally

One way to integrate ethical living into daily life is by adopting the mindset of thinking globally, acting locally. This means being mindful of global issues—such as climate change, poverty, and inequality—while taking action at the local level to address these challenges in practical ways. For example, supporting local farmers and sustainable businesses can help reduce the environmental impact of global supply chains, while volunteering in community projects can strengthen social bonds and contribute to the well-being of those around us.

- Voting with Our Dollars: One of the most powerful ways we can act ethically in a global context is by making conscious choices about where we spend our money. By supporting companies and organizations that align with our values—whether through fair trade practices, environmental sustainability, or ethical labor standards—we can contribute to a global economy that promotes human dignity and environmental stewardship.
- Advocating for Change: Beyond individual choices, ethical living also involves advocating for systemic change. This might mean supporting policies that

address climate change, campaigning for human rights, or promoting social justice initiatives. By using our voices and influence to advocate for a more equitable and sustainable world, we help create the conditions for global well-being.

Conclusion: A Connected and Ethical Life

Living a connected and ethical life involves recognizing our place within the global community and making choices that reflect our interconnectedness with all beings and the planet. Whether through acts of compassion, sustainable living, or effective altruism, ethical living allows us to contribute to the well-being of others and the environment, ensuring that our actions align with the values of unity and care.

Peter Singer's work on effective altruism offers a compelling framework for living ethically in a globalized world, reminding us that we have the power to make a positive impact on the lives of others, even those far beyond our immediate reach. By integrating these insights into our daily lives, we can help build a more just, compassionate, and sustainable world—one that reflects the oneness of all life.

Section 9.3: Service as Spiritual Practice

The ultimate expression of understanding the interconnectedness of all things is found in service to others. When we truly grasp that we are all part of a greater whole, it becomes clear that serving others is not an act of charity, but a reflection of our shared humanity—a way of affirming the oneness that connects us. In this sense, service becomes a spiritual practice, one that deepens our sense of purpose, fosters compassion, and allows us to live out the spiritual insight of unity.

Both Mother Teresa and Mahatma Gandhi embodied this philosophy of selfless service, seeing it as a path to spiritual growth and transformation. They believed that by serving others, especially the poor and marginalized, we come into closer alignment with the divine and experience the interconnectedness of life on a profound level. In this section, we will explore how service to others can be a powerful spiritual practice that helps us live more deeply connected and compassionate lives.

The Spiritual Power of Service

Service is often seen as something we do for others, but in the context of spiritual practice, it is much more than that. Service is a way of honoring the interconnectedness of all beings. When we serve, we are not merely helping others; we are recognizing that their well-being is intimately tied to our own. This understanding shifts the way we approach service, transforming it from a duty into a sacred act.

Service as an Expression of Oneness

When we recognize that all life is interconnected, serving others becomes a natural extension of that awareness. Helping others is not something separate from our spiritual lives; it is the living expression of the spiritual truth that we are all one. In serving others, we serve the whole—and in serving the whole, we serve ourselves.

- Seeing the Divine in Others: Many spiritual traditions teach that by serving others, we serve the divine. In Hinduism, for example, the concept of seva (selfless service) is rooted in the belief that the divine exists within every person. By serving others, we are serving God. Similarly, Mother Teresa often spoke of seeing Christ in the faces of the poor and sick, emphasizing that every act of service is an act of love for the divine in all people.

- Healing the Illusion of Separation: Service also helps to heal the illusion of separation that causes so much suffering in the world. When we serve, we break down the barriers between self and other, rich and poor, strong and weak. In the act of service, we affirm that we are all connected and that our well-being is bound up with the well-being of others.

Selfless Service in Action: The Teachings of Mother Teresa and Gandhi

Both Mother Teresa and Mahatma Gandhi dedicated their lives to selfless service, seeing it as a spiritual practice that not only helped others but also transformed themselves. Their teachings and actions provide a powerful example of how service can be a path to spiritual growth and an expression of the interconnectedness of all life.

Mother Teresa: Love in Action

Mother Teresa, who spent her life serving the poor and dying in the slums of Calcutta, often spoke of service as an act of love in action. For her, service was not just about addressing material needs but about recognizing the dignity and divinity of every person. She believed that every person, regardless of their circumstances, deserved love, respect, and compassion.

- Small Acts with Great Love: One of Mother Teresa's most famous teachings is that we do not need to do great things to make a difference; rather, we need to do small things with great love. She believed that even the simplest acts of service—offering a kind word, comforting the sick, feeding the hungry—are profound expressions of love and unity. These small acts, when done with genuine care and compassion, reflect the interconnectedness of all beings.
- Seeing Christ in the Poor: Mother Teresa often spoke of seeing Christ in the poor and in those she served. She believed that in serving the poor, she was serving God. This belief reflects the spiritual understanding that all life is sacred and that by serving others, we honor the divine presence in them.

Mahatma Gandhi: Service as a Path to Self-Realization

For Mahatma Gandhi, service was not only a way to help others but also a path to self-realization. He believed that true freedom and spiritual liberation could only be achieved through selfless service to others. Gandhi's philosophy of ahimsa (non-violence) and satyagraha (truth force) was grounded in the idea that serving others is the highest form of spiritual practice.

- Serving the Weakest: Gandhi taught that the measure of a society's greatness is how it treats its weakest members. He dedicated much of his life to serving the poor, the oppressed, and the marginalized, believing that by lifting up the most vulnerable, we uplift the whole of society. This reflects the understanding that we are all interconnected and that the suffering of one person is the suffering of all.
- Service as Self-Purification: Gandhi also saw service as a form of self-purification. By serving others without attachment to the fruits of the action, we purify the ego and align ourselves with the greater good. This idea of selfless service as a path to spiritual growth is central to many spiritual

traditions, including Hinduism, Buddhism, and Christianity.

Service as a Daily Spiritual Practice

While the examples of Mother Teresa and Gandhi are inspiring, service as a spiritual practice is not limited to grand gestures or lifelong dedication to humanitarian causes. Service can be integrated into our daily lives in small but meaningful ways. By adopting a mindset of service, we can make every interaction an opportunity to contribute to the well-being of others and to live out the spiritual insight of interconnectedness.

Practicing Service in Everyday Life

- Kindness in Daily Interactions: One of the simplest ways to practice service is by being kind and compassionate in our daily interactions. Whether at work, in our families, or in our communities, we can make a conscious effort to listen to others, offer help where needed, and treat everyone with respect. These small acts of kindness may seem insignificant, but they are powerful expressions of our shared humanity.

- Serving in the Community: Many people find fulfillment in volunteering or participating in community service projects. Whether it's helping at a local shelter, mentoring young people, or participating in environmental cleanups, these acts of service contribute to the greater good and foster a sense of connection to the wider community.

Service Without Attachment

A key aspect of service as a spiritual practice is to serve without attachment to recognition or reward. This idea, rooted in both Karma Yoga (the yoga of selfless action) and Gandhi's teachings, emphasizes that true service is done for its own sake, without seeking personal gain. By serving without expectation, we align ourselves with the flow of life and contribute to the well-being of others out of genuine compassion and love.

Conclusion: Serving Others as a Path to Oneness

Serving others is one of the most profound ways to live out the spiritual insight of oneness. When we serve, we recognize that the boundaries between self and other are illusions and that the well-being of all beings is interconnected. Whether through small acts of kindness or larger commitments to humanitarian causes, service becomes a powerful spiritual practice that helps us embody the values of compassion, unity, and love.

Both Mother Teresa and Mahatma Gandhi showed that service is not just an act of charity—it is a path to spiritual transformation. By dedicating their lives to the service of others, they demonstrated the power of selfless action to heal divisions, uplift the most vulnerable, and bring about greater harmony in the world.

As we integrate service into our own lives, we not only help others but also deepen our understanding of the interconnectedness of all life. Through service, we come to see that we are not separate from those we serve, but are part of a single, unified whole.

Chapter 10: Conclusion – The Infinite Journey

Section 10.1: Spiritual Growth as a Lifelong Path

As we come to the conclusion of this exploration of oneness, interconnectedness, and spiritual insight, it becomes clear that the journey of spiritual growth is not one with a final destination, but rather a continuous path—an infinite journey. The search for truth, meaning, and deeper understanding does not end with a single realization or moment of enlightenment; instead, it is a lifelong process, ever unfolding, and constantly inviting us to explore new dimensions of ourselves and the world around us.

In this sense, spiritual growth can be understood through the Taoist concept of the Way (or Tao), which represents the natural flow of life and the ever-changing nature of existence. In Taoism, the Way is not a fixed path with a clear endpoint but a dynamic, fluid process that is constantly in motion. The journey itself is as important as the destination, if not more so, because it is through the journey that we learn, evolve, and deepen our connection with the oneness of all things.

This final section reflects on the idea of spiritual growth as an endless quest, where every step, challenge, and discovery contributes to our ongoing awakening.

The Taoist Concept of the Way: A Path Without End

In Taoism, the Tao (the Way) is the fundamental principle that underlies all of existence. It is both the source of all life and the path that life follows. The Tao is often described as being beyond words and comprehension, yet it is also present in every moment and every aspect of the natural world. Lao Tzu, the legendary author of the *Tao Te Ching*, teaches that to live in harmony with the Tao is to live in alignment with the natural flow of life, accepting its changes and challenges as part of the ongoing journey.

Embracing the Flow of Life

The Taoist understanding of the Way reminds us that life is not a series of fixed events or outcomes but a continuous flow of experiences. Change and impermanence are intrinsic to the nature of existence, and spiritual growth requires us to embrace this ever-changing flow. Rather than striving for a final state of enlightenment or perfection,

Taoism encourages us to find peace and wisdom in the present moment, trusting that the journey itself is the teacher.

- Letting Go of Control: One of the key lessons of Taoism is the importance of letting go of control. Spiritual growth is not something we can force or master through sheer willpower. Instead, it involves surrendering to the flow of life, allowing ourselves to be guided by the Tao, and trusting that the path will unfold as it is meant to. This is often described as wu wei, or "actionless action"—the idea of acting in harmony with the natural world without forcing or resisting.
- The Journey as the Destination: In Taoism, the Way is both the path and the goal. The journey of spiritual growth does not have a fixed endpoint, because the process of learning, evolving, and awakening never ends. Each step along the path is valuable in itself, and every experience—whether joyful or challenging—offers an opportunity for growth. By embracing the journey as an essential part of the spiritual process, we come to understand

that there is no need to rush toward a final destination.

Spiritual Growth as a Lifelong Exploration

The idea that spiritual growth is a lifelong path is reflected in many traditions and philosophies beyond Taoism. Whether in Buddhism, Hinduism, or Sufism, the journey of awakening is seen as ongoing, with no definitive end point. Every new insight opens the door to further exploration, and every challenge serves as a catalyst for deeper understanding.

The Search for Truth and Meaning

The search for truth and meaning is one of the driving forces behind spiritual growth. This search, however, is not about finding definitive answers or achieving final enlightenment. Instead, it is about cultivating a deeper relationship with life's mysteries and learning to approach them with humility, curiosity, and openness. As we move through life, we encounter new questions, new challenges, and new opportunities for growth, each of which adds layers to our understanding of the world and ourselves.

- Accepting Uncertainty: A key aspect of spiritual growth is learning to embrace the uncertainty and mystery of life. The deeper we go on the spiritual path, the more we realize that there are no simple answers or clear resolutions. Instead of seeking to grasp and hold onto certainty, spiritual growth involves accepting the unknown and allowing it to guide us toward greater wisdom. This open-ended approach to life keeps us engaged in the process of learning and discovery.

- Learning Through Experience: True spiritual growth does not come solely from books or teachings; it comes from lived experience. Every experience we have—whether joyous or painful—serves as a teacher on the spiritual path. By reflecting on our experiences, practicing mindfulness, and staying connected to our inner wisdom, we learn and grow. This continuous learning process ensures that spiritual growth is dynamic and evolving, rather than static or final.

The Role of Patience and Persistence

Because spiritual growth is an infinite journey, it requires both patience and persistence. There will be times when the path feels difficult or unclear, when progress seems slow or elusive. However, these challenges are part of the process, and they often lead to the most profound insights. By remaining patient and committed to the journey, we cultivate the resilience and inner strength needed to continue growing, even in the face of obstacles.

Growth in Stillness and Struggle

Spiritual growth does not always happen in moments of clarity or inspiration. Often, it is during times of struggle, confusion, or even stagnation that the most important growth occurs. These moments force us to confront our limitations, let go of old patterns, and open ourselves to new ways of seeing the world.

- The Role of Stillness: Sometimes, the most profound growth occurs in stillness. By practicing mindfulness, meditation, or simply spending time in quiet reflection, we create space for inner transformation. This stillness allows us to listen more deeply to our inner guidance, to connect with the flow of life, and to recognize the subtle ways in which we are always growing and evolving.

- Persevering Through Challenges: Challenges and setbacks are inevitable on the spiritual path. Rather than seeing them as obstacles, we can view them as opportunities for growth. Every challenge teaches us something about ourselves—our strengths, our fears, our attachments—and gives us the chance to deepen our spiritual practice. By persevering through these difficult moments, we emerge with greater wisdom and clarity.

The Journey of Oneness: No Final Destination

The concept of oneness—the interconnectedness of all things—lies at the heart of spiritual growth. As we walk the path, we come to realize more fully that there is no separation between ourselves and the world, no division between the spiritual and the material. The journey of spiritual growth is, in many ways, a journey toward a deeper realization of this oneness.

Yet, even this realization of oneness is not a final destination. It is a living experience that continues to unfold, revealing itself in new and unexpected ways throughout our lives. Just as the universe is constantly expanding and evolving, so too are we continually deepening our understanding of the interconnectedness of life.

The Infinite Nature of Spiritual Growth

Because the universe itself is infinite, spiritual growth can never be complete. Every new insight, every moment of awakening, leads to further growth and transformation. The more we learn, the more we realize there is still to discover. This infinite nature of spiritual growth is what makes the journey so rich and meaningful. It keeps us engaged, curious, and open to the endless possibilities that life has to offer.

Conclusion: Embracing the Infinite Journey

As we conclude this exploration, it is important to remember that spiritual growth is not about reaching a final destination or attaining a fixed state of enlightenment. Instead, it is about embracing the journey—a journey that is infinite, ever-changing, and deeply interconnected with the flow of life.

The Taoist Way reminds us that the path itself is sacred, and every step along the way offers opportunities for growth, learning, and awakening. By cultivating patience, persistence, and openness to the unknown, we can live each day with a sense of wonder and gratitude for the ongoing journey of spiritual exploration.

Ultimately, the infinite journey is an invitation to live with mindfulness, compassion, and a deep respect for the interconnectedness of all things. As we walk this path, we honor the oneness that unites us all, and we contribute to the unfolding of a more harmonious, loving, and awakened world.

Section 10.2: Embracing the Unknown

As we move along the path of spiritual growth, one of the most profound challenges—and gifts—is learning to embrace the unknown. The mysteries of life and existence are vast, often defying rational understanding or explanation. Yet it is precisely in uncertainty and mystery that some of the deepest spiritual insights can be found. To walk a spiritual path is to acknowledge that we do not have all the answers, and that many of life's greatest truths lie beyond the reach of our intellect. It is through embracing this mystery and paradox that we open ourselves to deeper understanding and transformation.

The philosopher Søren Kierkegaard offers a powerful framework for approaching this uncertainty through his concept of the leap of faith. Kierkegaard understood that faith requires a willingness to step into the unknown, to trust in something greater even when the path forward is unclear. This leap of faith, along with the acceptance of paradox, can serve as a final call to embrace the mystery of existence with openness, trust, and humility.

The Mystery of Existence

From the beginning of human history, we have sought to understand the mystery of existence—why we are here, what the purpose of life is, and what lies beyond death. While science, philosophy, and religion offer different perspectives, there remains an unfathomable mystery at the heart of existence, one that resists easy answers or final explanations. Mystical traditions across cultures often point to this mystery as something to be experienced, not understood in a conventional sense.

The Limits of Rational Understanding

One of the greatest spiritual insights is the recognition of the limits of rational understanding. While reason and logic are invaluable tools for navigating the practical world, they cannot fully grasp the deeper mysteries of life. Concepts such as love, consciousness, the divine, and eternity often transcend the boundaries of human language and thought.

- Paradox and Duality: Many spiritual truths are expressed through paradox—statements that seem contradictory but point to deeper realities. For example, the idea that we are both individuals and part of a greater whole is a paradox that challenges our rational minds. In Taoism, paradox is embraced as a way of reflecting the dynamic nature of the universe, where opposites like yin and yang are not separate but interdependent aspects of the same reality.
- The Unknown as a Teacher: The unknown is not something to be feared but something to be

approached with curiosity and humility. By accepting that there are aspects of existence that we cannot fully understand, we allow ourselves to be taught by the mystery itself. This openness to the unknown invites moments of insight, intuition, and deep spiritual experience that can transform our understanding of the world.

Kierkegaard's Leap of Faith: Trusting in the Unknown

The Danish philosopher Søren Kierkegaard (1813–1855) famously described the journey of faith as a leap into the unknown. For Kierkegaard, true faith is not about certainty or having all the answers; it is about making a leap of trust, even when reason and logic cannot provide guarantees. This leap of faith requires us to let go of our need for control and certainty, and to place our trust in something larger than ourselves.

Faith as Risk and Trust

Kierkegaard's leap of faith is a risk, a stepping into the unknown without the assurance of a clear outcome. It is a moment of radical trust in which the individual chooses to believe in something beyond the limits of human reason—whether it is God, the divine, or the interconnectedness of all things. This act of faith is not based on evidence or certainty but on a deep inner conviction that transcends the mind's need for clarity.

- The Absurd and Paradox: Kierkegaard also spoke of faith as the embrace of paradox. He argued that true faith often involves believing in things that seem impossible or irrational from the perspective of reason. This embrace of paradox is what Kierkegaard referred to as the "absurd"—the realization that spiritual truths may defy logic but still hold profound meaning. For example, the Christian concept of God becoming human in the form of Jesus is, to Kierkegaard, an absurdity that faith can nevertheless accept as a deep spiritual truth.
- Letting Go of Certainty: The leap of faith requires us to let go of the need for certainty. In many ways, this is the ultimate act of spiritual surrender—trusting that the unknown holds meaning and purpose, even if we cannot see it. By stepping into the unknown, we open ourselves to a larger reality that transcends the limitations of our rational minds.

The Call to Embrace Uncertainty

In many spiritual traditions, there is a recognition that uncertainty is not something to be avoided or feared, but something to be embraced as part of the spiritual journey. The unknown invites us to explore deeper dimensions of existence, to move beyond our comfort zones, and to grow in ways we never imagined possible. By embracing uncertainty, we develop trust in the unfolding of life and in the wisdom that comes from not knowing.

Surrendering Control

One of the most profound aspects of spiritual growth is the willingness to surrender control. We are often taught to believe that we can—and should—control our circumstances, our future, and even our spiritual progress. But true spiritual insight comes when we recognize that much of life is beyond our control, and that surrendering to the unknown can lead to greater peace and understanding.

- Trusting the Process: Surrendering to the unknown does not mean giving up; it means trusting the process of life. It is about recognizing that we do not need to have all the answers to live a meaningful and fulfilling life. By trusting that life will unfold as it is meant to, we can let go of the anxiety that comes from trying to control every outcome and instead focus on being fully present in the journey.

- Letting Go of Expectations: Embracing the unknown also involves letting go of expectations—both of ourselves and of the spiritual path. Spiritual growth does not always follow a linear or predictable path, and the experiences we have may not match what we had envisioned. By releasing our expectations, we allow ourselves to be open to the unexpected gifts that the unknown can bring.

The Mystery as a Source of Wonder

Embracing the mystery of existence does not mean resigning ourselves to ignorance. On the contrary, it allows us to live with a sense of wonder and awe at the vastness of life. The unknown is a source of infinite possibility, inviting us to explore, learn, and grow without the need for certainty. In this way, the mystery of existence becomes a source of inspiration rather than a cause for fear.

Living with Wonder and Openness

When we approach life with a sense of wonder, we see the world not as something to be solved or conquered, but as something to be experienced and appreciated. This attitude of openness allows us to be more receptive to the beauty and interconnectedness of all things.

- The Unknown as Infinite Potential: The unknown is not just a void; it is a realm of infinite potential. By embracing the mystery of existence, we open ourselves to the possibility of new insights, experiences, and transformations. This openness to the unknown keeps the spiritual journey alive and dynamic, always inviting us to discover new dimensions of truth and meaning.
- Gratitude for the Journey: As we conclude this exploration, it is important to recognize the value of the journey itself. The spiritual path is not about reaching a final destination but about continuously exploring the unknown with gratitude and curiosity. Every step along the way, every moment of

uncertainty, contributes to our growth and deepens our connection to the oneness of all things.

Conclusion: The Leap into Mystery

As we reflect on the journey of spiritual growth, we are reminded that it is a path of embracing the unknown. The mystery of existence, with all its uncertainties and paradoxes, invites us to step beyond the limits of reason and into a deeper realm of trust and faith. Søren Kierkegaard's leap of faith teaches us that true spiritual insight often requires letting go of the need for certainty and embracing the mystery with open arms.

By accepting that we cannot know everything, we free ourselves to experience life more fully, with wonder, gratitude, and humility. The unknown becomes not a source of fear but a place of infinite potential, where new possibilities and insights await. As we continue on this infinite journey, may we have the courage to embrace the unknown, trusting that the mysteries of existence are part of the unfolding of a greater truth—one that connects us all in the web of life.

Section 10.3: Unity Through Diversity

As we bring this journey to a close, it is essential to reflect on one of the most beautiful and profound truths of the spiritual path: unity through diversity. The rich diversity of spiritual and philosophical traditions, practices, and perspectives is not a barrier to unity but rather a testament to the infinite ways in which the universal source manifests itself in the world. Each path, with its unique symbols, rituals, and teachings, contributes to the larger mosaic of human understanding, helping us to see that we are all connected, despite our differences.

Rather than seeing diversity as something that separates us, we can learn to view it as a celebration of the countless ways that truth, wisdom, and love are expressed. Every culture, religion, and philosophy offers its own window into the mystery of existence, and by embracing this diversity, we deepen our understanding of the oneness that lies beneath it all. As we navigate our own paths, it's important to honor the variety of traditions while recognizing the shared essence that unites them.

The Infinite Manifestations of the Universal Source

The universal source, or the underlying reality that mystics, scientists, and philosophers throughout history have sought to understand, is vast and beyond comprehension. It expresses itself in infinite forms, each of which offers a glimpse into the nature of existence. Just as a river has many tributaries that lead back to the same source, so too do the world's spiritual traditions offer diverse ways of approaching the same truth.

Diversity as a Reflection of Oneness

The diversity of spiritual and philosophical traditions reflects the richness of the human experience. Each tradition has developed in response to the unique cultural, historical, and environmental circumstances of the people who follow it. This diversity of expression is not a sign of division but a reflection of the oneness of life, manifesting in different forms to suit different contexts.

- Many Paths, One Truth: While the outward forms of spiritual traditions may vary—whether through different rituals, symbols, or teachings—they all point to the same universal truths: the interconnectedness of all life, the importance of compassion, the search for meaning, and the desire to transcend the limitations of the ego. By recognizing the shared essence of all traditions, we can celebrate the diversity of paths while honoring the oneness that unites them.

- **The Beauty of Different Perspectives:** Just as light refracts through a prism into a spectrum of colors, the universal source refracts through the lens of human culture into a spectrum of beliefs and practices. Each tradition offers a unique perspective on the divine, the self, and the cosmos, and by learning from these different perspectives, we enrich our own understanding of the spiritual path. Diversity is not something to be overcome but something to be cherished, as it reveals the many faces of the same universal truth.

Finding Your Own Path

In a world filled with so many spiritual and philosophical traditions, it is natural to wonder which path is the "right" one. But as we have explored throughout this journey, there is no single correct path to truth or enlightenment. Each individual's journey is unique, shaped by their own experiences, beliefs, and inner wisdom. The key is to find the path that resonates with your heart, while remaining open to the insights and wisdom that other traditions have to offer.

The Inner Path

Ultimately, the spiritual journey is an inner journey. While external practices and teachings can provide guidance, the real work of spiritual growth happens within. Each person's path will look different, and it is important to trust your own inner guidance as you explore different traditions and practices. Whether you find resonance in meditation, prayer, contemplation, or acts of service, the goal is to align with the truth of oneness and to live in a way that reflects that understanding.

- Trusting Your Own Experience: Spiritual growth is deeply personal, and what works for one person may not work for another. It is important to trust your own experiences and insights as you navigate the spiritual path. By listening to your inner voice and honoring your own process, you can find the practices and teachings that support your growth and help you connect with the deeper truths of existence.

- Remaining Open to New Insights: While it is important to trust your own path, it is equally important to remain open to the wisdom of other traditions. The more we expose ourselves to different perspectives, the more we can expand our understanding of the spiritual journey. Whether through reading sacred texts, participating in interfaith dialogue, or simply learning from the experiences of others, remaining open to new insights allows us to grow in wisdom and compassion.

The Shared Essence of All Traditions

Despite the diversity of spiritual and philosophical traditions, there is a shared essence that unites them all. At their core, most traditions emphasize the importance of love, compassion, humility, and service. They teach that the journey of spiritual growth is not about accumulating knowledge or achieving perfection but about cultivating a heart that is open, kind, and connected to the larger whole.

Unity in Love and Compassion

One of the most universal teachings across traditions is the importance of love and compassion. Whether in the teachings of Jesus, the Buddha, Confucius, or Rumi, we find a consistent message: love is the force that unites all beings, and compassion is the practice that brings us closer to the divine. When we live with love in our hearts, we reflect the oneness of all life, and when we act with compassion, we help to heal the divisions that separate us.

- Service as a Common Principle: As we explored in previous chapters, service is one of the most powerful ways to live out the understanding of oneness. Across all traditions, we find a call to serve others, to care for those who are suffering, and to contribute to the well-being of the community. By serving others, we align ourselves with the universal truth that we are all connected, and we live out the essence of what it means to be human.

Humility and the Recognition of Mystery

Another common thread in many traditions is the recognition that life is a mystery that cannot be fully understood or explained. This calls for humility in our approach to spirituality. No matter how much we learn or how deeply we explore the spiritual path, there will always be aspects of existence that remain beyond our grasp. By embracing the mystery with humility, we open ourselves to the infinite possibilities that life offers and allow ourselves to be continually surprised and inspired by the journey.

Conclusion: A Celebration of Unity and Diversity

As we conclude this exploration of spiritual growth and the journey of oneness, it is important to remember that diversity is not something that separates us but something that enhances our understanding of unity. The many paths, traditions, and perspectives that exist in the world are all part of the same tapestry of human experience, each contributing to the rich and complex story of our search for meaning.

Rather than trying to find a single, definitive path, we can celebrate the diversity of spiritual expression while recognizing the shared essence that unites us all. By honoring both the uniqueness of each tradition and the oneness that lies beneath them, we create a world where diversity is not a source of division but a source of strength and beauty.

As you continue on your own infinite journey, may you find inspiration in the many ways that truth is expressed. And may you live with the knowledge that, despite the differences in our paths, we are all walking together, united by the same universal source that flows through all of creation.

Glossary

Ahimsa

A principle in Hinduism, Buddhism, and Jainism meaning "non-violence" or "non-harming." It refers to a way of living that avoids causing harm to other beings, whether through action, thought, or speech.

Anatta

A Buddhist concept meaning "no-self," which teaches that there is no permanent, unchanging self. All things, including individuals, are in constant flux and are interconnected.

Compassion

A central spiritual and ethical principle across many traditions, compassion is the deep awareness of the suffering of others coupled with the wish to alleviate it. It is often considered an expression of the interconnectedness of all beings.

Effective Altruism

A philosophy and social movement popularized by philosopher Peter Singer, which encourages people to use their resources—such as time and money—to do the most good they can, particularly for global issues like poverty and animal welfare.

Fana

In Sufi mysticism, Fana refers to the "annihilation" or "dissolution" of the ego in the love of God, leading to a state of union with the divine.

Golden Rule

A universal ethical principle found in nearly all world religions, which states that one should treat others as one would wish to be treated. It is often seen as a foundation of moral conduct.

Interconnectedness

The concept that all beings and phenomena are deeply connected and dependent on each other, whether through relationships, ecosystems, or spiritual unity. It is a key teaching in both Eastern and Western mystical traditions.

Karma Yoga

A form of yoga in Hinduism that focuses on selfless service as a spiritual practice. It teaches that individuals should act without attachment to the results, dedicating their actions to the divine.

Leap of Faith

A concept from the Danish philosopher Søren Kierkegaard, referring to the act of trusting or believing in something without absolute proof, especially in the context of spiritual faith. It involves embracing uncertainty and paradox.

Mindfulness

A practice derived from Buddhist meditation that involves paying full attention to the present moment, without judgment. It is used to cultivate awareness, reduce suffering, and develop a deeper sense of connection with oneself and the world.

Mysticism

A spiritual tradition or practice that seeks direct experience or union with the divine, often through contemplation, meditation, or self-surrender. Mystical experiences typically emphasize the oneness of all things.

Nirvana

In Buddhism, Nirvana is the ultimate state of liberation from suffering, desire, and the cycle of birth and rebirth. It is the realization of the interconnectedness of all things and the dissolution of the ego.

Oneness

The understanding that all life is interconnected and that there is no separation between individuals and the greater whole. It is a central concept in many mystical and spiritual traditions, emphasizing unity and universal connection.

Paradox

A statement or concept that appears self-contradictory or illogical but contains deeper truth. Paradoxes are often used in spiritual teachings to express the complexity and mystery of existence.

Pratītyasamutpāda

The Buddhist doctrine of "dependent origination," which teaches that all phenomena arise in dependence upon other phenomena. Nothing exists independently; everything is interconnected.

Seva

A Sanskrit word meaning "selfless service." In Hinduism, it refers to the practice of serving others without expectation of reward, often as a spiritual offering.

Satyagraha

A term coined by Mahatma Gandhi meaning "truth force"

or "soul force." It refers to nonviolent resistance or civil disobedience in the pursuit of justice, grounded in the belief that truth and love are powerful forces for social change.

Tao

In Taoism, the Tao refers to the underlying principle of the universe, often translated as "the Way." It is the natural flow of life and existence, encompassing both the source and the path of all things.

Unity Through Diversity

A principle that recognizes the beauty and strength found in diversity, while emphasizing the underlying unity of all life. Despite differences in culture, belief, and practice, all beings are connected by the same universal source.

Wu Wei

A Taoist concept meaning "non-action" or "effortless action." It refers to living in harmony with the natural flow of life, acting without force or struggle, and aligning with the Tao.

Bibliography/References

1. **Capra, Fritjof.** *The Tao of Physics: An Exploration of the Parallels Between Modern Physics and Eastern Mysticism.* Shambhala Publications, 1975.
    - Explores the connections between quantum physics and the spiritual teachings of Eastern philosophies, emphasizing the interconnectedness of all things.

2. **Kierkegaard, Søren.** *Fear and Trembling.* Translated by Alastair Hannay, Penguin Classics, 1985.
    - A philosophical and theological work that introduces the concept of the "leap of faith" and the importance of embracing uncertainty in spiritual life.

3. **Lao Tzu.** *Tao Te Ching.* Translated by Stephen Mitchell, Harper Perennial, 1988.
    - A foundational text of Taoism that explores the Tao, or the Way, and emphasizes living in harmony with the natural flow of life.

4. **Singer, Peter.** *The Life You Can Save: Acting Now to End World Poverty.* Random House, 2009.
    - A work of ethical philosophy that presents the principles of effective altruism,

encouraging people to use their resources to make the greatest impact on global issues like poverty.

5. **Gandhi, Mahatma**. *The Essential Writings of Mahatma Gandhi*. Edited by Judith M. Brown, Oxford University Press, 1993.
    - A collection of writings by Gandhi, covering his philosophy of non-violence (ahimsa) and selfless service as a means of spiritual and social transformation.

6. **Mother Teresa**. *No Greater Love*. New World Library, 2002.
    - A collection of teachings and reflections by Mother Teresa on love, service, and seeing the divine in others, especially in those who are suffering.

7. **Hanh, Thich Nhat**. *The Miracle of Mindfulness: An Introduction to the Practice of Meditation*. Beacon Press, 1975.
    - A guide to mindfulness and meditation, emphasizing the importance of being present and fully aware in every moment.

8. **Smith, Huston**. *The World's Religions: Our Great Wisdom Traditions*. HarperOne, 1991.

- A comprehensive overview of the world's major religious traditions, exploring their core teachings and emphasizing the common spiritual themes they share.
9. **Rumi, Jalaluddin**. *The Essential Rumi*. Translated by Coleman Barks, HarperOne, 2004.
   - A collection of poems by the Sufi mystic Rumi, exploring themes of love, unity, and the divine connection that binds all beings.
10. **Thoreau, Henry David**. *Walden*. Princeton University Press, 2004.
- A reflection on simple living and the spiritual benefits of living in harmony with nature, emphasizing the importance of deliberate, mindful living.
11. **Eckhart, Meister**. *Meister Eckhart: Selected Writings*. Translated by Oliver Davies, Penguin Classics, 1994.
- A collection of writings from the Christian mystic, exploring the unity of the soul and God, and the process of inner transformation through the dissolution of the ego.
12. **Dalai Lama and Desmond Tutu**. *The Book of Joy: Lasting Happiness in a Changing World*. Avery, 2016.

- A dialogue between two of the world's spiritual leaders on the nature of joy, compassion, and interconnectedness.

13. **Anonymous**. *The Cloud of Unknowing*. Translated by Carmen Acevedo Butcher, Shambhala Publications, 2009.
- A classic work of Christian mysticism that emphasizes the importance of embracing the mystery of God and approaching the divine through love rather than intellectual understanding.

Printed in the USA
CPSIA information can be obtained
at www.ICGtesting.com
CBHW030410301024
16599CB00050B/472